DYNAMICS OF EZRA POUND'S POETRY

DYNAMICS OF EZRA POUND'S POETRY

HARI SHARAN LAL

AUTHORSPRESS

Worldwide Circulation through Authorspress Global Network
First Published 2009
by
Authorspress
E-35/103, Jawahar Park
Laxmi Nagar, Delhi-110092
e-mail: authorspress@yahoo.com

Dynamics of Ezra Pound's Poetry
ISBN 978-81-7273-485-5

Printed in India at Tarun Offset, Delhi.

Dedicated to

the loving memory of

my mother

(Late) ***VASANTI DEVI***

And it is presented to my wife

VEENA

who is always a

source of my

strength

vigour

and determination

Preface

Pound is an uncompromising and meticulous artist in craft of writing. But his reputation as a poet has suffered because of his political stances, his dislike of contemporary academic community, and his criticism of Protestant Christianity. Pound has suffered because of his extreme ideological, cultural, and socio-economic views. Nevertheless, he has generally been recognized as a bold experimenter and a great influence on modern poetry.

What needed, is an unprejudiced study and assessment of Pound's poetic achievements. His poetic career extends over a long period, 1905-1972 and he has written too much in the fifty years of his poetic career. An examination of his total poetic output is a stupendous task. Pound can, therefore, best be studied in phases of his career. My investigation of Pound's poetry is concerned with his yearly poetry as well as the poems published during 1920-1930, and the Cantos, the most ambitious work of art that Pound published in many decades. The period is well defined by the first world war before it and the great economic crisis at the end of it. The literary movements and intellectual and critical ideas in which Pound was involved, had a direct bearing on his poetic creations.

The book is an attempt to study Pound's poetry in the light of his relevant critical ideas. His poems are analyzed with reference to the themes they express and the situations they present. Some textural elements such as imagery, tone, rhythm and shades of meanings have also been discussed. This composite approach to individual poems is intended to elucidate the nature of experience.

The first two chapters briefly outline the state of Pound's scholarship and his literary theories and critical ideas which were a by-product of, and an aid to creative activities. Pound's early poetry aroused a mixed reaction. There were adverse comments on his recondite themes and dense allusions, but the sincerity of expression in these poems won praise. Likewise there has been a mixed reaction in respect of *Hugh Selwyn Mauberley* and *A Draft of XXX Cantos*.

Pound's preoccupation with the principles of Imagism and his definition of the poetic image as a liberating force from space limit and time limit are closely linked with his poetic creations. Soon he gets interested in Vorticism and the concept of kinetic image. In Pound Vorticism becomes a theory of energy in poetry concerned with the principles of shape, relationship between words and emotions, and use of precise visual images. Pound dissociated himself from Imagist "movement" because he found in it the excess of fixed images. From Vorticism, too, he went a step ahead and became pre-occupied with the Chinese ideogram.

He learnt about the Chinese ideogram from Fenollosa's paper on Chinese characters, which bore an analogy to the technique of poetry. Pound's study of Japanese poetry, especially haiku, led him to the theory of superpository technique of deploying images. His view of the Chinese ideogram enabled him to employ juxtaposition of images in his longer poems and the *Cantos*. In short, Pound's involvement with the theories of Imagism, Vorticism, and Chinese ideogram was aimed at achieving objectivity and a minimum claim for personality in the composition of a poem. Pound was also interested in the use of myth as a technique of expressing moods and psychic experiences. His adaptation of the Ovidian metamorphoses was concerned with the transformation of mythical characters to express the harsh realities of life. Pound's formulation of all these critical theories were relevant to his poetry and met his creative need.

Chapter-III presents an investigation of Pound's early poems, published in *Umbra* (1920). The collection contains poems composed during 1908-1912, poems which he wanted to keep in circulation during the 1920's. These poems are predominantly lyrical and manifest the influence of Arnaut Daniel, Cavalcanti, Browning, W.B. Yeats, Swinburne, and Morris; and they are all marked by Pound's modernist sensibility and technique. The novelty discernible in these early poems is carried over into his later poetry, too, although he added something more to it as he grew. In the poems of *Umbra,* his creative translations and adaptations from Provencal and Italian poets, too, evince his modernist contributions and novelties. In these poems, written in a variety of poetical forms, Pound experiments with the device of employing personae as his masks. The poems are marked by speech rhythm and objective presentation of reality and states of consciousness. Technically speaking, they were as relevant to the 1920s as when they were written.

Chapter-IV discusses the main characteristics of those poems of *Personae* (1926) which were composed during 1912-1920 and which he reprinted to keep in circulation because they were relevant in the context of the literary scene in the 1920s. These poems reflect Pound's critical preoccupations with Imagism, Vorticism and the Chinese ideogram – ingredients of modernist poetic. They present a bewildering variety of modes and illustrate Pound's concern with technique, translations, objectivity, concreteness and lucidity. There are also satirical poems which bear the influence of Catullus, Martial and Gautier. The poems examined are marked by proper idioms, presentation of ideas with clear images, precise facts, and sophisticated ironic rendition. Satirical tone, ideographic images, multiple personae, and the art of objective presentation – these pave the way for an understanding of the Cantos.

Chapter-V analyses *Hugh Selwyn Mauberley,* a poem composed and published for the first time in 1920. An attempt is made to understand its themes and discuss the problems of structure and unity. The poem is a serious work of art which presents the critical and alarming situation of the times. In the first section there are thirteen poems, in the second only five. But the poem as a whole deals with the themes of literary hollowness, cultural aridity, and social chaotic conditions. Its themes and moods provide the unifying links. The *Envoi*, the last poem of the first section, is a lyric, and its vision of beauty is again reinforced in the last poem of the second part. But the poem, on the whole, is satirical, attacking both the establishment and the aesthete unable to cope with the situation. It is lit up with dark humour and ironic portraits of literary figures. Allusions, references and translations incorporated in the poem bring alien sensibility to provide an objective criticism of the first two decades of the twentieth century. The poet, in short, diagnoses the cause of the ailments of the modern age and, at the same time, evokes the cult of beauty to serve a point of contrast.

Chapter-VI discusses Cantos which gathers up the themes and techniques perfected in the poems studied in the earlier chapters and uses them in a complex whole of epic dimensions. A complex usage of personae, ideograms, rhythms and images, and mature art combine to express a complex and rich mind and sensibility. Some of the Cantos which gather up the themes and techniques perfected in the poems studied in the earlier chapters use them in a complex whole of epic dimensions. Some of the Cantos read like condensed miniature epics. They deal with the western culture unrolled by a history and put into Homeric and Dantean scaffolds. The Homeric framework of the Cantos expresses the theme of quest, and the Dantean scaffold presents the values of society under the perspective of Inferno, Paradise and Purgatory. The structure of the poem can also be seen as rooted into Pound's theory of triplex-fresco, and psychological analogy.

The Cantos present, thus, history, quest theme, and a hierarchy of values. They are a combination of continuous and discontinuous forms, and subjective and objective facts of history. Pound's use of myths and the metamorphosis present complexity objectively. There is a variety of themes, experiences and episodes, which are presented in terms of contrast and similitude. The Cantos expand into an encyclopaedic form, with satirical edge and cultural criticism.

The poems examined demonstrate Ezra Pound's masterly craftsmanship, involvement with European culture, and knowledge of human situations and human conditions. Pound's contribution to modern poetry is great. His poetry and criticism are integrated which lend authority to each other; he has put many a modern poet under his debt.

His poetry has a wide range; it is individualistic as well as social, lyrical as well as satirical, epigrammatic as well as encyclopaedic. Ezra Pound may be said to be the inventor of twentieth century poetry and the poets' poet in the real sense.

Ezra Pound is universally acknowledged as a writer of immense learning and great eminence. It was Conrad Aiken who introduced T.S. Eliot to Pound in 1915. He published *Prufrock* in *Poetry* and launched Eliot's poetic career. He also helped him get his first volume of poems published by the Egoist Press, in 1917; and in 1922, Eliot placed the manuscript of a sprawling and chaotic poem, called, *The Waste Land* that Pound reduced about half its size. Eliot dedicated his poem to Pound and for his 'blue pencilling' – called him *il miglior fabbro,* the master craftsman.

Like Irving Babbit Pound taught people right doctrines for producing great literature. For half a century, Pound has been a teacher and protector of great poets of modern age. The great writers like T.S. Eliot, W.B. Yeats, Hemingway and Tagore have expressed their indebtedness to Pound. Pound chose all art for his province. He wrote verse and prose; composed music and was a great painter and a fine sculptor. He studied Theophile Gautier, Propertius, Arnant Daniel, Dante, Cavalcanti, Stendhal, Flaubert, Remy de Gourmont, Confucius, Fenollesa and Homer.

Ezra Pound is a poet of a higher and rare order. The present book will certainly provide new directions in the field of research on Pound and the students and research scholars will be able to understand Pound's poems and critical ideas in right manner. Most of Pound's famous and difficult poems are explicated and analysed coherently. In most of the universities in India and abroad, Pound is a part of the syllabus of English and American Literature.

I hope that the study of Pound's Poetry and Poetics elucidated in the book, will help the students and scholars, locate and discover the 'real Pound' who revolutionized and activated the whole of the twentieth century literature.

9th Feb, 2009 **Hari Sharan Lal**

Acknowledgements

I want to express my gratitude to (Late) S.M. Pandeya, former Professor of Comparative Literature, Department of English, Banaras Hindu University, Varanasi, India. His scholarly guidance on Pound helped me in right perspective. I also acknowledge my debt to Dr. K.L. Goodwin, former Professor, Department of English, Queensland University, Queensland, Australia, for giving his scholarly suggestions. I also wish to thank my reverend teacher Professor V.K. Chari, Professor of English, Carlton University, Canada, who provided research materials on Pound and exhorted me to work hard.

My debt to published scholarship is amply acknowledged in notes and Bibliography.

"His (Pound's) writing had layers of meaning, but it is not ambiguous. It's scale of values would have been understood by Dante, Chaucer and Langland.... It deals with the perennial struggle of man's creative intelligence against the exploiters of the abundance of nature."

William Cookson

Contents

1

Introduction

Ezra Pound (1885-1972) is a scholar-poet who has written extensively in verse and prose. His writings have been analysed, criticized, and evaluated by men of diverse critical persuasions in the form of reviews, essays, monographs, and scholarly works. Much of this criticism has been the result of irritation caused by Pound's poetry, which bristled with recondite themes, terse diction and experimental techniques. Pound's merit has remained eclipsed and, in his life-time, he suffered much from agreement and disagreement of critics.

The first poetical work of Pound *Personae* (1909) published in England, aroused a mixed reaction. Its poems appeared to be puzzling and problematic to critics of the period. Edward Thomas remarked:

> Let us straightway acknowledge the faults; the signs of conflict; the old and foreign words and old spellings that stand doubtless for much that the ordinary reader is not privileged to detect; the tricky use of inverted commas; the rhythms at one time so free as not to be distinguishable at first from prose, at another time so stiff that 'evanescent' becomes evanescent....[1]

Thomas notes the nature of Pound's diction accurately but he ends with that. The second collection of poems *Exultations* (1909), which contained Pound's creative translations from Provencal, Italian, Latin and old English, was not welcomed either. Edward Thomas, again, reviews the collection in subdued irritation:

> It is a relief to us to turn from all but meaningless suavity and skill to something that appears to be individual. And doubtless no ordinary man could or would write like Mr. Pound. But having allowed the turbulent opacity of his peculiarities to sink down we believe that we see very nearly nothing at all.[2]

Thomas, in spite of his admiration for certain lyrics, feels baffled on the whole.

Edwin Muir found *Umbra* (1920) fastidious, full of obscure forms, and reconditure themes. But he appreciated the sincerity of Pound and the expressiveness of his poems.[3] *Cathay* (1915) and *Lustra* (1916), containing translations from Chinese, Latin, and Provencal did not fare any better than the earlier volumes. Some of the poems were satirical, and some epigrammatic. His transcreations were taken for literal translations. Consider, for example, W.G. Hale's remark:

> If Mr. Pound were a professor of Latin, there would be nothing left for him but suicide. I do not counsel this. But I beg him to lay aside the mask of erudition. And, if he must deal with Latin, I suggest that he paraphrases some accurate translations, and then employ some respectable students of the language to save him from blunders which might still be possible.[4]

W.G. Hale fails completely to see the poems as poems; he rather sees them as literal translations. May Sinclair shows a better perception of the poems; he finds in them "clear hardness", "civilized polished beauty", and "Augustan irony".[5]

When *A Draft of XVI Cantos* appeared, it evoked negative criticism, because the critics could not see any structure.[6] W.B. Yeats, in his Introduction to *The Oxford Book of Modern Verse* (1936), noted the complexity and obscurity of the Cantos. His comments offer valuable insight into the real nature of the poem that was still in the process of seeking its form and ended with the death of the poet.

> Ezra Pound has made flux his theme; plot, characterization, logical discourse, seem to him abstractions unsuitable to a man of his generation. He is mid-way in an immense poem in *vers libre* called for the moment *The Cantos*, where the metamorphosis of Dionysus, the descent of Odysseus into Hades, repeat themselves in various disguises, always in

> association with some third that is not repeated.... There is no transmission through time, we pass without comment from ancient Greece to modern England, from modern England to medieval China, the symphony, the pattern, is timeless, flux eternal and therefore without movement.[7]

Yeats discussed the uncompleted Cantos with suspended judgment. He made insightful comments on the fragments that made up the published Cantos; at that stage of their progress, they lacked form. Earlier, in 1928, Yeats had felt disturbed by Pound's puzzling theory of the fresco analogy and mathematical structure.[8] He did not see any form in the published twenty-seven cantos as a whole.

Although Yeats's observations are valuable for anybody who wants to pursue a serious study of Pound's Cantos. Second-rate critics were quick to lift isolated phrases from his observations and used it against Pound, misused the authority of Yeats.

Louis Zukofsksy doubted the genuineness of the construction of the Cantos and its division into Inferno, Paradise and Purgatory. He found the poem without "poetic intensity."[9] The most scathing criticism of Pound's poetry came from R.P. Blackmur who remarked in 1934:

> Mr. Pound is neither a great poet nor a great thinker. Those of his followers who declare him the one only belittle him, and when he writes as the other, he belittles himself.[10]

R.P. Blackmur felt dissatisfied with fragmentary and non-discursive growth of Pound's Cantos; and poems like *Hugh Selwyn Mauberley* appeared superfluous and disintegrated, as there appeared no logic and no argument.[11] Blackmur is intelligent enough to understand the logic, but he cannot rise to read satires on his culture. That is why, perhaps, he finds Pound at his best in his translations. Raymond Mortimer, Sir Maurice Bowra, and Robert Graves, always felt unhappy with Pound's poetic creation.

An appraisal of Pound's poetry in the right direction has, however, come from T.S. Eliot, who has written seven times on Pound, *Ezra Pound: His Metric and Poetry* (1917), "Note on Ezra

Pound," (*Today*, IV, 19 Sept. 1918), "The Method of Ezra Pound," (*The Athenaeum*, 46669, October 1919); "Isolated Superiority," (*Dial*, Jan. 1928), Introduction to *Selected Poems* (1928); "Ezra Pound," (*Poetry*, LXVIII, Sept. 1946); and Introduction to the *Literary Essays of Ezra Pound* (1968). Eliot has also made some observations on Pound's hell Cantos in *After Strange Gods* (1934), which shows his Anglican point of view that is contrary to Pound's concept of Confucian morality.

T.S. Eliot treats Pound as the most serious poet and justifies his art of verse, use of Personae, Translation, form and content. T.S. Eliot also accepts Pound's great influence on other poets, including himself. The contemporary poets have not only cultivated their sensibility but also improved their sense of poetry writing under the influence of Pound's poetry. When *Personae* (1926) came out, T.S. Eliot found in the poems an "exquisite sense of humour," masterly "epistolary style," and apt use of images. On the Cantos Eliot has remarked:

> The only criticism which could be made of the Cantos is that Pound's auditory sense is perhaps superior to his visual sense. His eye is indeed remarkable, it is careful, comprehensive, and exact; but it is rare that he has an image which combines the precise and concrete with a kind of almost infinite suggestion.... I know that Pound has a scheme and a kind of philosophy behind it; it is quite enough for me that he thinks he knows what he is doing; I am glad that the philosophy is there, but I am not interested in it.[12]

Eliot perceives in the Cantos a greater operation of the auditory sense than the visual. Why is it, one may wonder, that Eliot's own later poetry is more auditory than visual? Somewhat like Yeats, he is silent on Pound's structure. Perhaps he too did not perceive any form in the Cantos. He accepts the possibility of structure on Pound's authority, as the possibility of an underlying philosophy. He finds Pound's originality genuine; his sense of life penetrates the life of other ages as well as his own.[13] T.S. Eliot also finds in Pound's poetry a developing phase of colloquial tone. In Pound's poems, there is a great personal involvement, which is seen in the development of technical accomplishment in most of his poems. Pound's translations appear original "through him and he finds himself through the original."[14] *Hugh Selwyn Mauberley* is great in poetic craftsmanship, variety of verse, positive sensibi ity, and criticism of life at large.[15]

Hugh Selwyn Mauberley (1920) being compa ratively easier than the Cantos has attracted a number of critics, 'hose criticism still fail to solve the problem of its structure. Nonetheless John J. Espey, George Dekker, Rosenthal, A.L. French, Walter Sutton, Edith Sitwel, Hoffman, Herbert N. Schneidau, F.R. Leavis, Hugh Witemeyer and Hugh Kenner have studied the poem according to their own points of view. Pound's major poetic work, his *Cantos*, has been studied by Harold Watts, Noel Stock, Lewis Leary, Clark Emery, George Dekker, Walter Baumann, and Daniel Pearlman. These critics deal with several aspects of the *Cantos*, including the problem of its structural unity and the unifying theme. Noel Stock denies any "principle of unity" in the first thirty cantos and finds the poem full of complexities.[16] George Dekker studies the theme of Eros. Daniel Pearlman makes a sincere effort to explore out a principle of unity in Pound's Cantos.[17]

Pound is a scholar poet, and in his poems there is a deep personal involvement which goes on developing with his exploration of different forms of poetry though he never changed his principles as a person. He started his poetic career with a good knowledge of European, Chinese, Italian and Provencal literatures and had enough enthusiasm to look for newness in literature and art. His classicism showed a concern with the permanence of literature manifested in the best poets of different ages. His search for variety and experience is a continuous quest for poetic truth. The fifty years of his poetic life displays development in craftsmanship as well as consistency in his principles. His early poems collected in *Umbra* (1920), present his apprenticeship which enabled him to forge out an adequate form of language, as a medium for objective presentation of feelings.

REFERENCES

1. Edward Thomas, "Two Poets," *Ezra Pound: The Critical Heritage*, ed. Eric Homberger (London: Routledge & Kegan Paul), p. 50.
2. Edward Thomas, "The Newest Poet," *The Critical Heritage*, p. 61.
3. Edwin Muir, "New Age," *Ezra Pound: The Critical Heritage*, p. 196.
4. W.G. Hale, "Pegasus Impounded," *Poetry*, XIV (April 1919), pp. 54-55.
5. May Sinclair, "The Reputation of Ezra Pound," *North American Review*, CCXI (May 1920), p. 668.
6. Glenway Wescott's Review in *Dial*, LXXXIX (December 1925), p. 502.
7. William Butler Yeats, quoted in Ezra Pound: *A Collection of Critical Essays*, ed. Walter Sutton (Englewood Cliffs: Prentice-Hall, Inc., 1963), p. 9.
8. W.B. Yeats, "A Packet for Ezra Pound," *Ezra Pound: A Critical Anthology*, ed. J.P. Sullivan (Harmondsworth: Penguin Books Ltd., 1970), p. 100.
9. Louis Zukofsksy, "Ezra Pound," *Ezra Pound*, ed. J.P. Sullivan, pp. 114-15.
10. R.P. Blackmur, *Language as Gesture* (London: George Allen & Unwin Ltd., 1954), p. 124.
11. *Ibid.*, p. 126.
12. T.S. Eliot, "Isolated Superiority," *Dial*, 84 (Jan.-June 1928), pp. 5-6.
13. T.S. Eliot, "Introduction," *Selected Poems of Ezra Pound* (London: Faber and Faber, 1928), pp. 10-11.
14. *Ibid.*, p. 13.
15. *Ibid.*, p. 20.
16. Noel Stock, *Reading the Cantos: A Study of Meaning in Ezra Pound* (London: Routledge and Kegan Paul, 1967), p. 10.
17. Daniel Pearlman, *The Barb of Time: On the Unity of Ezra Pound's Cantos* (New York: Oxford University Press, 1969), p. 20.

2
Finding a Poetics

At the time when Pound started writing, the cultural situation in the English-speaking world was deplorable. There was a lack of any coherent critical theory, and the poets were left to the old devices. It is in this situation that Pound ventured upon new aspects of poetry and literary criticism. He laid down critical principles to guide contemporary poets and writers. He exercised great influence on the technique and treatment of subjects in poetry.[1] He wanted to see poetry free from vague generalizations and thought that good writing should be interpretative and have the virtues of good prose with austere and direct elements.[2]

As a conscious artist, Pound presents certain norms in his Poetics drawn from his knowledge of many languages, cultures, and traditions. This made him the most important poet of his time in English Language.[3] T.S. Eliot has acknowledged his indebtedness to Pound:

> I have, in recent years, cursed Mr. Pound often enough; for I am never sure that I can call my verse my own; just when I am most pleased with myself, I find that I have only caught up some echo from a verse of Pound's. . . . Pound's critical influence is immense, and beneficial. (I wish he would let me edit his critical essays, instead of doing it himself.) My own critical debt to him is as great as my debt in versification.[4]

Pound wanted to see a band of creative writers who could act as "guide and lamp of civilization."[5] Pound's studies lent him an "aesthetic fastidiousness," "technical perception," and "exquisite eclecticism."[6] He pointed out the necessity of knowledge of different languages for comparative investigation of literary traditions. He found the contemporary criticism and poetry in a deplorable condition. He remarks:

> Every critic should give indication of the sources and limits of his knowledge. The criticism of English poetry by men who knew no language but English, or who knew little but English and school-classics, has been a marasmus.[7]

To teach, to move, and to delight have been the permanent ends of poetry.[8] With this conception in mind, Pound endeavoured for the improvement of the literary arts. The criticism which might improve the arts was valuable:

1. The critic most worth respect is the one who actually causes an improvement in the art he criticizes.
2. The best critic of next rank is the one who most focuses attention on the best work.
3. The pestilence masking itself as a critic distracts attention from the best work, either to secondary work that is more or less "good" or to tosh, to detrimental work, dead or living snobbisms, or to indefinite essays on criticism.[9]

Criticism should be used for the preparation of good writing.

In order to bring an improvement in the use of language in poetry with precision, Pound put forth a threefold principle in 1912:

1. Direct treatment of the 'thing' whether subjective or objective.
2. To use absolutely no word that does not contribute to the presentation.
3. As regarding rhythm; to compose in the sequence of the musical phrase, not in a sequence of a metronome.[10]

This theory is directed towards a search for adequate language. Pound wanted to achieve objectivity in expression, in the presentation of facts and ideas. Pound emphasizes the virtues of direct and austere language:

> As to Twentieth century poetry, and the poetry which I expect to see written during the next decade or so, it will, I think, move against poppy-cock, it will be harder and saner, it will be what Mr. Hewlett calls 'nearer the bone'. It will be as much like granite as it can be, its force will lie in its truth, its interpretative power (of course, poetic force does always rest there); I mean it will not try to seem forcible by rhetorical din, and luxurious riot. We will have fewer painted adjectives impeding the shock and stroke of it. At least for myself, I want it so, austere, direct, free from emotional slither.[11]

Pound opposed the use of interjections, flying words, clichés, stereotyped journalese, "hind-side beforeness," "straddled adjectives," and rhythms without meaning. On the positive side, he stressed objectivity as the sole factory to bring perfection in literature. Language of poetry was an offshoot of "concrete things," and he advised poets not to use "general expression" because it dulls the effect of communication.[12]

Imagism was a method of dispersonalization of emotions because for the presentation of ideas an Image was the best medium. Pound particularly emphasized the art of presentation and condensed expression. His definition of image has psychological depth:

> An 'Image' is that which presents an intellectual and emotional complex in an instant of time. I use the term 'complex' rather in the technical sense employed by the newer psychologists, such as Hart, though we might not agree absolutely in our application.
>
> It is the presentation of such a 'complex' instantaneously which gives that sense of sudden liberation; that sense of freedom from the limits and space limits; that sense of sudden growth, which we experience in the presence of the greatest works of art.
>
> It is better to present one Image in a lifetime than to produce voluminous works.[13]

The psychological aspect of Image relates to the Freudian concept of action being impelled by emotion and systematic ideas linked up with each other in the subconscious mind. The term "complex" suggests an active force in the presence of a "stimulus" that occurs when one or more ideas combine. The psychological theory of the complexes refers to obsessions, whereas Pound's concept intends the normal process and presentation. His main concern is to capture ideas and feelings in instants or moments and present them with definite values. A poet, in presenting objects and situations, registers emotions adequately and exactly and manifests them objectively. Presentation of images, whether conceptual or perceptual, should aim at producing clarity of vision and recognition of meaning in the object. Efforts should be made to find particulars in similar things, and universals in particulars. This assumption of the particular in the universal and the universal in the particular leads to a desirable conception of poetry which inspires Pound's own poetry. Pound's views of images is intended to outline the morphology of experience. The doctrine can be conveniently illustrated with reference to his poem *In a Station of the Metro.*

Ezra Pound dissociated himself from Amy Lowell's Imagism in 1914 and shifted to Vorticism. Imagism as understood by Lowell seemed to him unable to present visual images. Vorticism was a kind of advancement on Imagism. It was a movement, launched by Wyntham Lewis in 1914. Its main characteristics were those of the formalist and abstract painting and sculpture. Vorticism reflected machine-like consciousness and dealt with a kind of energy. In his pursuit of the vorticist image Pound associated himself with Wyndham Lewis, and Gaudier-Brzeska. The movement was also directed against the bourgeois concept of art.

The vortex issue of *Blast* made the following announcement in 1914:

> Sculptural energy is the mountain.
>
> Sculptural feeling is the appreciation of masses in relation.
>
> Sculptural ability is the defining of those masses by planes.[14]

The sculptural energy, feeling, and ability were given great emphasis. Pound called the vortex a "magnetic rose pattern" of creative energy. He defined the poetic image in vorticist terms:

> The image is not an idea. It is a radiant node or cluster; it is what I can, and must perforce, call a VORTEX, from which, and through which, and into which, ideas are constantly rushing. In decency one can only call it a VORTEX. And from this necessity came the name "vorticism". *Nomina sunt consequentia rerum*, and never was that statement of Aquinas more true than in the case of the vorticist movement.[15]

Pound, in his vorticist analogy, considers energy a vital force of creation. Energy is shapeless, and the job of the poet is to give it a shape. The emotional energy in the consciousness of the author is the primary form; it takes a visual form marked by intensity, efficiency, and visibility of pigments. Vorticism laid emphasis on the use of moving images. For Pound, an image, in the vorticist context, becomes a medium of presentation of concrete things. He wrote to Berry: "It is as simple as the sculptor's direction: Take a chisel and cut away all the stone you don't want."[16] The energy of poetry is present in the sound, music, and arrangement of words. The peculiar characteristics of the arrangement of images consist of visual and verbal dynamism. One can observe the fixity in flux and flux in fixity. Language "charged with meaning to the utmost possible degree"[17] is related to the theory of energy.

The vorticist's denial of imitative art led Pound to the Chinese ideogram in 1916. He tried to find out ideographic roots of words and the verbal idea of action. This discovery was useful to Pound in presenting images after images in long poems like the Cantos. Pound studied Chinese pictograph in the British Museum, and came to look upon the Chinese language as an ideographic language. He found, in Chinese, the syntax of words almost in motion. Pound read Fenollosa's essay on the *Chinese Written Character* and found aesthetics of good writing in it. He worked on Fenollosa's notes and found that the Chinese characters rendered the "perceptive reality," a kind of peculiar structural device, metaphor, and ideogram were interlinked with each other. He developed Fenollosa's notes into an essay and, as its co-author, stressed the utility and cultural tenets of Chinese and Japanese literatures and their social traditions. He dealt with the Chinese language, the problem of verb, its role in the communication of meaning, and presentation of an image:

> One superiority of verbal poetry as an art rests in its getting back to the fundamental reality of time. Chinese poetry has the unique advantage of combining both elements. It speaks at once with the vividness of painting, and with the mobility of sounds. It is, in some sense, more objective than either, more dramatic. In reading Chinese we do not seem to be juggling mental contours but to be watching things work their own fate.[18]

In the same article some of the main characteristics of sentence-construction were elaborated as found in the Chinese and the English language. Pound stressed the role of the metaphor and verbal idea of action in a sentence:

> Poetry is finer than prose because it gives us more concrete truth in the same compass of words. Metaphor, its chief device, is at once the substance of nature and of language. Poetry only does consciously what the primitive races did unconsciously. ... that the greatest strength of one language lies in the splendid array of transitive words, drawn both from Anglo-Saxon and from Latin sources. These give us the most individual characterization of force.[19]

A long poem, according to Pound, should present a "phalanx of particulars." His concept of the ideogrammic method in poetry centred around a major stylistic device. Particular and general ideas have to be juxtaposed. The genuineness of Poundian ideogram has been questioned by several critics, who only find a kind of misunderstanding.[20] Nonetheless Pound discovered in it a "kind of seeing," perceiving clear ideas in a visual manner. Ideogram consists in a visual perception of presented ideas in contrast. It is a kind of "making," of presenting ideas with pictures. Ideographs are used as metaphors. A technique that evolves out of the ideogram consists of a kind of reprise, i.e. action, or praxis in the plot of the poem. The Poundian ideogram in its summary form, may be presented in a diagram:

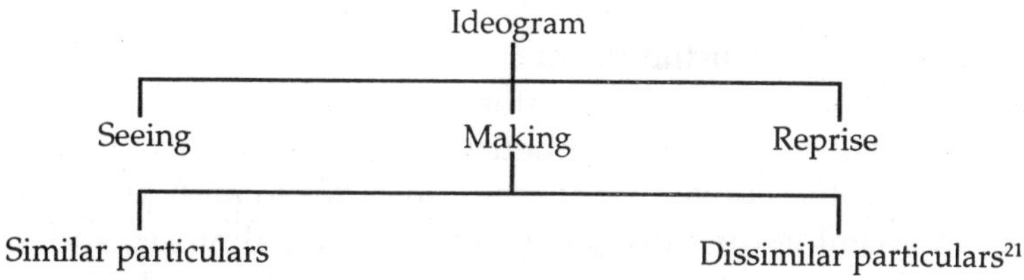

The Aristotelian principle of mimesis, action, metaphor, etc. appears in the above diagram. Pound, in order to find out an equation of emotion, uses the idea as an image which passes through the processes of Imagism, Vorticism, and Ideogram. The ideogram deals with metaphor, and the metaphor starts towards the ideogram. Because in the ideogrammatic style, the idea of action or making is not possible without the use of concatenations of metaphor.[22]

Pound's various theories amount to a poetic programme. As a critic and poet his main task was to achieve objectivity. He studied poetry, analysed its properties, and tried to formulate certain principles of art. He classifies the properties of poetry as Melopoeia, Phanopoeia and Logopoeia:

> MELOPOEIA, wherein the words are charged, over and above their plain meaning, with some musical property, which directs the bearing or trend of that meaning.
>
> PHANOPOEIA, which is a casting of images upon the visual imagination.
>
> LOGOPOEIA, 'the dance of the intellect among words'. That is to say, it employs words not only for their direct meaning, but it takes count in a special way of habits of usage, of the context we *expect* to find with the word, its usual concomitants, of its known acceptances, and of ironical play. It holds the aesthetic content which is peculiarly the domain of verbal manifestation, and cannot possibly be contained in plastic or in music. It is the latest come, and perhaps most tricky and undependable mode.[23]

Melopoeia deals with the musical properties of a poem. The rhythm and sound effect, through untranslatable, can be enjoyed even by one who does not have the knowledge of the language in which the poem is written. Music in a poem is inevitable. No good poet can afford to dispense with it. Because when there is no music, poetry wastes its beauty. Pound renounced the conventional metre in order to shift attention "from accent to quantity as a function in verbal music, and to classical meter in their diversity... He was able to enlarge the repertoire of poetic rhythms and acquired conversational rhythms.[24] The conversational rhythm is free from the metronomic pattern. It consists of "musical phrases."

Rhythm is an essential part of the poem and depends on the variation of tone and the frequency of pitch. Pound's melopoeia also deals with indispensability of sound which is produced by alliterative usage and rhymes, assonance, immediate rhyme and delayed rhyme, and simple and polyphonic sound. Melopoeia charges language with meaning. Pound was a master of verse forms and made others improve their "verse sense."[25]

Phanopoeia dealt with images, created by the visual imagination of the poet. Unlike melopoeia, it is translatable. The use of visual images in a line or two brings precision. Images, when the generalized notions of meanings are discarded, stand for particular conceptual value. The Chinese ideograph belongs here. Phanopoeia presents directness and clarity and, as such, it is related to concept of ideogram. The Imagist theory, as Northrop Frye has remarked "made a great deal of the pictorial element in the lyric, and many imagistic poems could almost be described as a series of captions to invisible pictures."[26] Phanopoeia adheres to this conception of the image, which stands as objective expression of an idea. Frye finds Pound's technique of phanopoeic and melopoeic presentation to be a kind of lyricizing.

Pound makes a clear distinction between bad diction and good diction, between rhetoric and logopoeia. Pound uses logopoeia not for direct meaning, but for ironical modes of expression. It can employ words for intellectual connotation and express the attitude of the mind as well. Connotative logopoeia of this kind is suited for satire. The intellectual handling of words facilitates wit and humour. Pound describes satire as "surgery, insertions and amputations."[27] He considers Laforgue the best satirist of his time, because he used good verbalism, good logopoeia. He gives a list of writers who were good satirists of their time, and in whose writings he sees logopoeic usage. They have hardness, ironical expression, good verbalism, and sharp-edged attack on the evils of society. Logopoeia can stimulate the associations (intellectual and emotional) that have remained in the receiver's consciousness in relation to the actual words or word groups employed.[28]

Hugh Selwyn Mauberley is satirical in mode, and its logopoeia adequately presents effective verbal allusions. In "Irony, Laforgue, and Some Satire" he prefers "delicate irony," which is intelligent employment of words. It is the role of the ironist to make the reader "think."[29] Logopoeia makes the readers think; words as a precise medium of expression, are forced from the association of other meanings.

The threefold components of poetry just discussed above enter into Pound's method and style. They inspire and become a part and parcel of his own technique. In short, melopoeia deals with the auditory qualities such as tone and sound; phenopoeia is a kind of verbal composition with visual characteristics of words; and logopoeia reverberates with meanings associated with customs and other references. Pound thinks that in logopoeia Eliot surpasses him and he surpassed Eliot in melopoeia.[30]

Pound's critical insights establish some correlations between modernity and the past. The study of past literature broadened his vision and enabled him to acquaint himself with the best traditions and forms of creative writing. According to Pound, the main task of an artist is to see perfection by treating literature at par with the scientific subjects. Science aims at precise and exact communication of facts. In his opinion "the serious artist is scientific in that he presents the image of his desire, of his hate, of his indifference as precisely that, as precisely the image of his own desire, hate or indifference. The more precise his record the more lasting and unassailable his work of art."[31] But in addition to scientific presentation Pound has tried to discover the art of maximum efficiency of expression and newness. For this, a writer has to find out established truths which exist in the domain of knowledge and which he should try to apply in his own art. Tradition, for Pound, presents a concept of beauty, preserved in literature.

Pound examines five categories of criticism. They are criticism by discussion, criticism by translation, criticism by exercise in the style of a given period, criticism via music, and criticism in new composition. Pound shows interest in "criticism by translation" and "criticism in new composition"[32] The two functions of criticism are to "forerun composition" and to accomplish "excernment." It stands for ordering the material and the removal of repetition. Pound defines criticism as "the ordering of knowledge so that the next man (or generation) can most readily find the live part of it, and waste the least possible time among obsolete issues."[33] Such a conception of criticism is, obviously, directed towards new creation.

"Criticism by translation" belongs to excernment method, because the translation of best works has to present a kind of selection. Excernment, similarly enables a critic to select the best works, and to add new works to the list. In this manner, the language of literature can progress and improve. Selection helps in the discovery of newness. This sense of discovery is concerned with Pound's concept of the traditions of the Medieval, Chinese, Greek, and Roman literatures. Pound's excernment method can be seen in two of his works, *The Spirit of Romance* and *I Gather the Limbs of Osiris*.

According to Pound, Homer, Chaucer, Dante, and the melic poets are such writers who illuminate other poets of other languages in different periods of culture.[34] He likes Homer for his "authentic cadence of speech," his singing quality, suggestions of "poetic motions," and his auditory imagination. History is a part of tradition and Pound deals with the Chinese, Renaissance, Greek, western, and modern history. T.S. Eliot is indebted to Pound in his concept of tradition. Tradition gives a writer a vision of pastness of the past and its relation to present as well.[35] Pound's view of objective history and the historical sense is remarkable:

> The history of an art is the history of masterwork, not of failures, or mediocrity. The omniscient historian would display the masterpieces, their causes and their inter-relation.... All ages are contemporaneous. It is B.C., let us say in Morocco. The Middle Ages are in Russia. The future stirs already in the minds of the few. This is specially true of literature, where the real time is independent of the apparent, and where many dead men are our grandchildren's contemporaries, while many of our contemporaries have been already gathered into Abraham's bosom, or some more fitting receptacle.
>
> What we need is a literary scholarship, which will weigh Theocritus and Yeats with one balance, and which will judge dull dead men as inexorably as dull writers of today, and will, with equity, give praise to beauty before referring to an almanack.[36]

History in Pound's poems presents certain values and constantly searches order and disorder, the permanent and the trivial, which are posited in terms of contrast and give a structure to ironic situations. He defines the epic as that which contains history. It is not necessary, for a poet, to have a systematic form, a beginning, a middle and an end. The vastness of the experience, however, has to be presented in a convincing manner. Pound's concept of history blends with his views of myth and tradition. Myths are objectified realities of human history and communicate experience. They are a process of humanization of gods and goddesses and express human mood:

> I believe in a sort of permanent basis in humanity, that is to say, I believe that Greek myth arose when some one having passed through delightful psychic experience tried to communicate it to others and found it necessary to screen himself from persecution. Speaking aesthetically, the myths are explications of mood: you may stop there, or you may probe deeper. Certain it is that these myths are only intelligible in a vivid and glittering sense to those people to whom they occur.[37]

In the passage just cited Pound defines myth as a method of expression. Myths are explications of mood. This is a kind of psychological theory of myth. In another context Pound looks upon myths as verbal equations of emotion. This conception is related to the psychological view, but the emphasis falls on "verbal equations." The story of the hero of a myth becomes the persona of the myth-maker and presents the experience in an objective manner. The concept of myth that Pound enunciates is very much applicable to his own poetry. Poetry for Pound is an art of verbal presentation of experience. His equation theory is illuminating and applicable to both myths and poetry:

> Poetry is a sort of inspired mathematics, which gives us equations, not for abstract figures, triangles, spheres, and the like, but equations for the human emotions. If one have a mind which inclines to magic rather than to science, one will prefer to speak of these equations as spells or incantations; it sounds more arcane, mysterious, recondite. Speaking generally, the spells or equations of "classic" art invoke the beauty of the normal, and spells of "romantic" art are said to invoke the beauty of the unusual.[38]

Pound was always interested in the problems of the art of communication, and he discovered equation for communication in different modes. The word "magic" in above citation refers to metamorphosis, in which things are often magically changed. Gods and goddesses metamorphose themselves, and their transformation communicate the experience of suffering, agony, or ecstasy. Sometimes an unusual experience cannot be communicated; the mythical mode, at this juncture, helps the poet in communication of ideas. The mythical episodes do not claim authenticity as historical details. They belong to structures of emotion and belief. In myths one can find not only his emotional satisfaction but also additions to knowledge. A poet objectifies his experience in mythical presentation, and thus, myths "interplay between *poiema* and *logos*."[39]

Metamorphosis is also concerned with myths, and Pound has given great importance to Ovid's *Metamorphoses*. In Ovid, mythical episodes of gods and goddesses establish metamorphic traditions. Lucius Apuleius' *Golden Ass* is an important book of metamorphic stories. But Pound prefers Ovid to Lucius. The Latin version of Ovidian metamorphic stories opens the vista of Roman culture and folklore.[40] In metamorphoic context characters or things change, but they do not perish. A goddess changes into a tree, and a god may change into an animal shape. These transformations communicate objective values of human emotions of love, greed, fear, and lust. Persephone, Demeter, Artemis, and Daphne appear in Pound's poems and are found changed into animate and inanimate objects. The stories of their change convey an experience.

Myths which project immoral activities of lust and sex indulgence present archetypal human situations. But fables that register the psychic experience express moods. The metamorphic principle becomes a structural device in Pound. His personae are transformed. The speaker of the poems reveals the truth of the mythical character. Fables, drawn from different mythologies, are mixed and are made to present objective realities of life. Myth and metamorphosis form a method of impersonal presentation of experience in Pound.

Study of personae is also an important device in achieving objective presentation of emotion and experience. Pound shows his concern with the technique of persona from the beginning of his career:

> I began the search for the real in a book called Personae (1909), casting off, as it were, complete mask of the self in each poem. I continued in a long series of translations, which were but more elaborate masks.[41]

Pound's translations, too, give him an opportunity to use a variety of masks expressing the self, objective reality and, states of consciousness.

The mask or the persona in the translated poem arises, as it were, from the ashes, speaks in a voice contemporaneous with the original poet, and throws light on manners, men, and modes of social living of his time. His concerns and criticism become relevant to the modern situation as well. Pound's translations present a historical background and make the reader acquainted with the technical forms of past languages. Pound's translations are imaginative creations, not literal renderings. They are adaptations, paraphrases, transliterations, and translations combined together.

Pound's sense of ethical and moral order is influenced by his study of Chinese literature, particularly of Confucius and Mencius. In his essays *Immediate Need of Confucius and Mang Tsze,* Pound deals with values. In the first essay, he points out the debasement in western ethics, a kind of ill-health caused by exploitation, and a defective system of money. Pound finds usury even in religion. He attacks Christian religion, especially Catholicism, and treats of Christian virtues as hypocritical. In his opinion, "civilization consists in the establishment of an hierarchy of values, it cannot remain as a mere division between the damned and the saved ..... with alternate wailing and hysterical merriment.[42] Pound finds money value, in the form of commercialization, always interfering in the field of art and literature. Usury appears to Pound a great evil, a great source of human suffering. The Christian concept of hell, Pound felt, was imaginary. For him Paradise and Inferno exist on earth. Pound's political and economic views, his admiration of fascism and condemnation of usury and jewry, led to his torture by American "patriots." His views still arouse strong feelings in many.

Ezra Pound's poetic programme is inspired by a number of valuable critical theories, and his reputation as a critic is lasting. His practical criticism, is instructive as well as constructive. The programme was of immense guidance to Pound and other poets of his generation. He wrote a number of poems with his critical standards. The theory of image and language had a fecundating effect of his poetry. Pound's critical principles were directed towards writing poetry.

REFERENCES

1. K.L. Goodwin, *The Influence of Ezra Pound* (London: Oxford University Press, 1966), p. 204.
2. Patricia Hutchins, *Ezra Pound's Kensington: An Exploration, 1883-1913* (London: Faber and Faber, 1965), p. 132.

3. Sisir Kumar Ghosh, "Ezra Pound," *Span*, XIV, 12 (1973), p. 29.
4. T.S. Eliot, "Isolated Superiority," *Dial*, 84 (Jan.-June 1928), pp. 5-7.
5. *The Selected Letters of Ezra Pound, 1907-41*, ed D.D. Paige (London: Faber and Faber, 1959), p 48.
6. F.R. Leavis, *New Bearings in English Poetry* (Harmondsworth: Penguin Books Ltd., 1963), p. 117.
7. *Literary Essays of Ezra Pound*, ed. T.S. Eliot (London: Faber and Faber, 1968), p. 56.
8. *Ibid.*, pp. 77-78.
9. *The Selected Letters of Ezra Pound*, p. 241.
10. *Literary Essays of Ezra Pound*, p. 3.
11. *Ibid.*, p. 12.
12. *The Selected Letters of Ezra Pound*, p. 49.
13. *Literary Essays of Ezra Pound*, p. 4.
14. Quoted in Charles Norman, *Ezra Pound* (London: Macdonald, 1969), p. 151.
15. Ezra Pound, "Vorticism," *F-ortnightly Review*, XCVI (1914), pp. 69-70.
16. *The Selected Letters of Ezra Pound*, p. 91.
17. *Literary Essays of Ezra Pound*, p. 23.
18. Ernest Fenollosa and Ezra Pound, "The Chinese Written Character as a Medium for poetry," *Little Review*, VI, 5 (Oct., 1919), p. 61.
19. *Ibid.*, p. 58.
20. Ben D. Kimpel and T.C. Duncan Eaves, "Pound's Ideogrammic Method," *American Literature*, LI, 2 (May 1979), pp. 207-08.
21. Hugh Kenner, *The Poetry of Ezra Pound* (London: Faber and Faber, 1951), pp. 76-105.
22. *Ibid.*, pp. 87-91
23. *Literary Essays of Ezra Pound*, p. 25.
24. T.S. Eliot, "Isolated Superiority," *Dial*, 84 (Jan.-June 1928), pp. 1-2.
25. William McNaughton, "Ezra Pound's Meter and Rhythm", *PMLA* (1963), p. 130.
26. Northrop Frye, *Anatomy of Criticism: Four Essays* (Princeton: Princeton University Press, 1957), p. 275.
27. *Literary Essays of Ezra Pound*, p. 45.
28. Ezra Pound, *ABC of Reading* (London: Faber and Faber, 1934), p. 63.
29. *Literary Essays of Ezra Pound*, pp. 281-82.

30. *Ezra Pound Selected Prose 1909-65*, ed. William Cookson (London: Faber and Faber, 1973), p. 291.
31. *Literary Essays of Ezra Pound*, p. 46.
32. *Ibid.*, pp. 74-76.
33. *Ibid.*, p. 75.
34. *Ezra Pound, Selected Prose 1909-65*, ed. William Cookson, pp. 25-29.
35. T.S. Eliot, *Selected Essays* (London: Faber and Faber, 1969), p. 14.
36. Ezra Pound, *The Spirit of Romance* (London: Peter Owen, 1970), pp. 7-8.
37. *Ibid.*, p. 92
38. *Ibid.*, p. 14.
39. R.L. Brett, *An Introduction to English Studies* (London: Edward Arnold Ltd., 1965), p. 33.
40. *Ezra Pound, The Spirit of Romance*, pp. 14-18.
41. Ezra Pound, "Vorticism," *Fortnightly Review*, XCVI, 573 (Sept. 1, 1914), pp. 463-64.
42. *Ezra Pound: Selected Prose 1909-65*, ed. William Cookson, p. 104.

3

The Early Poetry 1908-12: The Search for a New Aestheticism

Umbra (1920) contained a selection of Ezra Pound's early poems which he wanted to keep in circulation. These poems were drawn from his earlier volumes: *Personae* (1909), *Exultations* (1909), and *Ripostes* (1912). In addition, *Umbra* contained translations from Guido Cavalcanti and Arnaut Daniel and poems of T.E. Hulme. These poems were written with a conception of poetry which was incorporated in his theory of Imagism in 1912. Pound's first collection of poems appeared as *A Lume Spento* (1908) and contained fourteen poems. Of these eight poems were reprinted in *Personae* (1909), and three in *Exultations* (1909). The rest of the poems were dropped out. Christine Brooke-Rose considers *Umbra* a "mixed bag."[1] But all of them illustrate Pound's early conception of poetry and his aestheticism.

When Pound appeared on the scene of English poetry, writers were in search of craft, sentiment, vision, and sincerity.[2] F.S. Flint noticed in *Personae* (1909) a sense of revolt against the mode of conventional poetry. He also felt that some poems carried echoes and traditions of Browning, medieval poets and W.B. Yeats.[3] Edward Thomas, in his review of the volume, liked Pound's art of "directness and simplicity."[4] *Exultations* (1909) contained translations and adaptations from Provencal, Italian, Latin, and old English. Flint found in them a kind of picturesque presentation and vague beauty. Pound's poems were written in a variety of verse forms which defied the use of conventional regular metrical beat and rhyme.[5] *When Ripostes* (1912) appeared, Pound was recognized as a poet of revolt. His poems demonstrated his effort to achieve conversational, real, and contemporary tone. The appearance of *Umbra* (1920) made Edwin Muir comment on the recondite themes and the difficult form. But he had to admit the "artistic purity"[6] of Ezra Pound.

The critics generally see the poems of *Umbra* as falling into two groups. The poems of 1908-1910, which seem to have been written in the aesthetic tradition, show his adoption of different models and deal with unfamiliar themes and obscure forms. But the poems written in 1912 deal with contemporary subject matter. Pound's aestheticism carries the influence of the Pre-Raphaelite poets and of W.B. Yeats and Browning. His translations are adaptations from the Provencal and early Italian poetry. Pound's interest in the medieval world aims at the revival of the art and forms of medieval poetry. The hints of aestheticism are found in the quotations, allusions, and direct references. But his main concern in the early poems is to produce beauty, which does not belong to the spiritual and philosophical mysticism of Morris, Pater, and Wilde. It is unlike Platonism, too.[7] T.S. Eliot, however, traces out the influence of Swinburne, Yeats, Morris, and Browning on Pound's early poems, particularly on their manner and style. In the later works of Pound, this influence remains as an emotional attitude.[8]

Pound is a poet of great technical accomplishments; and although it is easy to trace out different influences on Pound, he made his way towards modernism from the very beginning of his poetic career. *Umbra* selects only such early poems as Pound thinks need circulation in 1920 in the context of the modernist movement in poetry. Pound lays emphasis on good writing "as opposed to the opalescent word, the rhetorical tradition."[9] Herbert N. Schneidau connects Pound's idea of good writing with Ford Madox Ford's concept of presentation, which meant registration of the form of an experience. This aim dominates the Imagist poetry: each poem seeks to register an experience, an emotion, or a state of mind with what might now be called "presentational immediacy."[10]

Pound's preoccupation with form was encouraged by his study of the Romance languages, medieval literatures, and Provencal poetry. It sharpened his insight into myth, metamorphosis, sound, and rhythm. He learned Canzoni verse form of Arnaut Daniel and found it relevant to modern ears. From the Troubadours he learnt the art of interpretation and exact presentation.[11] If the Provencal studies enabled him to know of the cult of emotion, the Tuscan poets made him to know of the cult of the harmonies of the mind, and the Renaissance presented him with a "cult of cultures."[12] His translations and adaptations, in *Umbra*, yield perceptions of "the technical development of the art of poetry."[13] This enabled Pound to do the new thing in the right direction. The critical ideas which are presented in *The Spirit of Romance*, deal with facts of good prose, visual images, scientific precision, and rhythm.

From Provencal poetry Pound learned the use of mask and equip himself with form and idiom to express an experience adequately. The mask became Pound's "persona". His translations were a useful technical exercise in the use of mask. Pound's personae, in his early poems, were a conscious technical experimentation with the poet:

> ... in the search for "sincere self-expression," one gropes, one finds some seeming verity. One says, "I am" this, that, or the other, and with the words scarcely uttered one ceases to be that thing.
>
> I began this search for the real in a book called *Personae* (1909), casting off, as it were, complete masks of the self in each poem. I continued in a long series of translations, which were but more elaborate masks.[14]

The poems of *Umbra* (1920) circulated from *Personae*, (1909), *Exultations*, (1910), and the translation of Canzoni's, sonnets, etc. bear witness to the primary influences on the poet. He learnt the technical device of using personae at the very beginning of his career.

Apart from it, Pound's appreciative attitude towards Swinburne, Rossetti, and the Decadents throws some light on another aspect of his poetry. At the time he began to write he found that a relevant tradition of poetry did not exist in England and America. Hence, in a letter, he advised his friend William Carlos Williams to look to good poets for stimulus and inspiration:

> If you'll read Yeats and Browning and Francis Thompson and Swinburne and Rossetti you'll learn something about the progress of Eng. poetry in the last century. And if you'll read Margaret Sackville, Rosamund Watson, Ernest Rhys, Jim G. Fairfax, you'll learn what the people of second rank can do, and what damn good work it is. You are out of touch. That's all.[15]

Pound likes Browning's *The Ring and. the Book,* which contains the various experiments of Robert Browning. Browning's works have lyrical, dramatic and narrative elements in them. But Pound chiefly appreciated Browning's use of the monologue, conversational diction, and psychological insight. The poetry of Swinburne is marked by its verbal music. Swinburne and Oscar Wilde present a vision of beauty close to Paganism.

Wilde and Swinburne revolted against Victorianism which presented "pomposity, respectability and hypocrisy."[16] The Pre-Raphaelite idealization of woman corresponded, in Pound's mind, to that he found in the Provencal poetry. Rossetti introduced Pound to the mystic world of medievalism, especially Tuscan poetry. The Pre-Raphaelites and Yeats stimulated Pound's interest in the idea of pure art. Pound liked Symons and the Decadent poets for their resentment against rhetorical use of language in poetry. Symons appreciates the qualities of Mallarme:

> "Poetry", said Mallarme, "is the language of a state of crisis"; and all his poems are the evocation of a passing ecstasy, arrested in mid-flight. This ecstasy is never the mere instinctive cry of the heart, the simple human joy or sorrow.... It is a mental transposition of emotion or sensation, veiled with atmosphere, and becoming as it becomes a poem, pure beauty.... The pure work, then, implies the elocutionary disappearance of the poet, who yields place to the words, immobilized by the shock of their inequality; they take light

> from mutual reflection, like an actual train of fire over precious stones, replacing the old lyric afflatus or the enthusiastic personal direction of the phrase.[17]

Pound's main tenets of the art of poetry are close to Symons' description of Mallarme's art. In short, Pound's imaginative faculty from 1908 to 1911 was constantly developing towards the preparation of modernism of 1912. But the early period carried certain influences which mark the peculiar structure of his poems.

Some of the poems in *Umbra (Cino, Na Audiart, Famam Librousque Cano*, and *La Fraisne)* were first published in *A Lume Spento* in 1908, and reprinted in *Personae* (1909). They carry the influence of Browning as well as the Provencal poetry. They also contain dramatic elements. In a letter to William Carlos Williams, Pound wrote about his poems:

> To me the short so-called dramatic lyric—at any rate the sort of thing I do – is the poetic part of a drama, the rest of which (to me the prose part) is left to the reader's imagination or implied or set in a short note. I catch the character I happen to be interested in at the moment he interests me, usually a moment of song, self-analysis, or sudden understanding or revelation. And the rest of the play would bore me and presumably the reader. I paint my man as I conceive him. Et voila tout.[p18]

In this observation two things come up. The first thing that appears is Pound's art of presenting the character. He chooses his persona to suit his point of view. The second thing concerns the element of dramatic ecstasy and diction. The art of presenting the dramatic persona is akin to Browning's art of presenting the persona. Browning's persona bristled with intellectual clothing. Pound, however, does not allow his persona to spoil the poetic intensity by didactic meanderings. The use of the monologue, rendered in musical phrases, expresses the internal mental conflict. Pound presents the inner blurring of the character. His characters are poets, jongleurs and lovers, and they belong to the tradition of Browning's art of Persona.

Cino, written in 1909, is a monologue. The poem's epigraph "Italian Campagna 1309, the open road," refers to the Italian poet Cino da Pistoia, who had gone into exile. Similarly, a mention of other poets is made in *Marvoil* and *Piere Vidal Old. Cino* contains details from the life of Cino Da Pistoia and begins with a colloquial tone:

> Bah: I have sung women in three cities,
>
> But it is all the same;
>
> And I will sing of the sun.[19]

The Persona of *Cino* is a wanderer, and its theme is similar to that in Arthur Symon's poem *Wanderer's Song*. The protagonist of Arthur Symon's poem feels attracted by the "white road," but the opening lines of Pound's poem suggest Browning's way of expression in a monologue.[20] The first strophe, consisting of three lines, has the features of a soliloquy. Cino da Pistoia, was a friend of Dante, and wrote a number of poems dealing with his love for Bolognese lady. His poems possess the traditional vein of Tuscan love poetry and use the form of monologue, rendering a psychological state. In 1307, Cino went into exile, and stayed with Philipo Vergio Lesi, who had a daughter, Selvagia. The poet, after his banishment, became a wanderer. He had no comfort at all. The epigraph as well as the opening refers to Walt Whitman's *Song of the Open Road* to Symon.

The protagonist of *Cino* wanders from city to city and meets women after women. The opening strophe makes three statements addressed to the audience. The lines refer to the experience of the speaker. Cino had bitter experiences in the exile. His experience of woman and his suffering as a companionless man are presented with conflicts of emotion. The speaker presents a dream world which does not exist for long. The use of "lips," "dreams," "night," etc. refers to the pleasure that the protagonist had in the company of ladies. The persona, afterwards, changes his position; Cino is presented as "passionate Cino," "frail Cino," "Gay Cino," "a saucy fellow," and "Lackland Cino," etc.. The mood of the poem undergoes a change and Cino speaks in elliptical language about woman:

"...eh? ... they mostly had grey eyes." The poem ends with three lines stating his resolution to "sing of the road with sun and birds". The directness appears in lines:

> I will sing of the white birds
> In the blue waters of heaven,
> The clouds that are spray to its sea.
>
> (*EPSP*, p. 35)

Cino presents the reminiscences of a wanderer and deals with his associations with beautiful ladies. The experience presented has remarkable lyric intensity. The speaker's consciousness evokes a feeling for beauty and the pleasure it yields. Disillusioned with women he turns to the beauty of nature, which serves a point of contrast.

The title of poem *Famam Librosque Cano* means "I sing of fame and books." The persona of the poem is endowed with a gift for poetic creation, which seems a sufficient reason to bring him fame. The poem is marked by a conversational note. The poem elliptically begins with a question: "Your songs?" The opening is dramatic and suggestive. The tone, to some extent, becomes ironic, and the narrative is marked by the use of appropriate uncouth words. Direct ejaculations in "Ah-eh ! the strange rare name.../Ah-eh ! He must be rare if even I have not...." make for emotional intensity. The discontinuity of the syntax is occasioned by this intensity. The sentences deliberately destroy the monotony and uniformity of traditional rhythm. Thomas Jackson, however, considers this a defect in the lift of conventional rhythm and verse:

> Here Pound's long, tortuous sentences, issuing in a series of floating clauses connected only obscurely with any grammatical subject, are characteristic of Browning, and so are the semantic exigencies that apparently necessitate this obscurity of syntax: most often the detached and interjected clauses and phrases are modifications of the main clause, ... so that – and this is characteristic of Browning's sentences— the particular relevance of each part to the whole does not become apparent until the end.[21]

Jackson's comparison of Pound with Browning is right, but he fails to see that the suspended resolution of the syntax until the very end serves to lay emphasis on the immediacy of experiences.

Famam as well as *Cino* manifest some features of the Browningesque monologue and persona in the preceding pages mark the starting point of his own persona. In *Cino,* there are shifts in the point of view from Cino to that of women and back of Cino. But in both the poems the speakers are Pound's personae. Pound's personae appear in four types of poems: (1) the translations, (2) poems very close to Pound's models which use a mask, (3) poems in which Pound is speaking through someone, but they are not monologues, (4) the more or less consistent dramatic monologues which, even when they voice the words of a poet, go beyond mere translation.[22]

The title of *Marvoil* refers to the Provencal poet Arnaut de Mareuil. The speaker of the poem presents the character of the poet from the Provencal poetry who acts like a Browningesque figure because he is seen speaking in colloquial tone. The protagonist, the Italian poet, supplies facts and truths of his real life; he was dismissed from the court of the Vicomte de Beziers. Arnaut de Mareuil wrote many songs in which he praised the Countess of Beziers. But when Alphonso II took the throne and became the king of Aragon, the poet was banished from the Court and was sent into exile. In this poem, the protagonist, Morvoil, is sitting in a cheap tavern, and when he is asked about his identity, he says:

> A poor clerk I, 'Arnaut the less' they call me,
> And because I have small mind to sit
> Day long, long day cooped on a stool
> A-jumbling o'figures for Maitre Jacques Polin,
> I ha' taken to rambling the South here.
>
> (*EPSP*, p. 49)

Pound presents Marvoil's physical appearance and mental agony in colloquial idiom. The second part of the poem presents facts about his love for the Countess of Beziers. The third part shows Arnaut's hatred of the King of Aragon. The fourth strophe shows his deep love for the countess and the next three parts of the poem deal with the jongleur, a hole in the wall of the tavern, and the secrecy of love that he keeps in his breast. Pound's poem does not exactly tally with the original *Canzoni*. There are many changes. In his Canzone, Arnaut de Mareuil never showed his detestation of Alphonso, king of Aragon.

Pound, in general, presents the characteristics of a Troubadour poet. He makes his protagonist show his complex obsession with love, manners of love letters, boldness, timidity, and suffering.[23] The speaker is a historical figure. The use of the monologue in the poem deals with mere events. The poem deals with the theme of the poet; contemporary modes and manners of Vida appear authentically. Pound presents the poet's passion as a lover, and his concern with his professional craftsmanship. Arnaut de Mareuil appears as a courtier, a professional writer, and a poet. As a clerk he could not earn his bread. Dejected and disappointed, he left the job and became a wanderer. The presentation of the speaker in the line "Day long, long day cooped on a stool" shows the simplicity of Pound's art of presentation of the character. The speaker shows his resolution of love and describes his divine experience of the "first kiss." The facts of history, in glimpses, present the cult of Provencal culture. Pound uses the events of the life of Arnaut de Mareuil as historical facts. He makes them interpretative.

W.B. Yeats finds an echo in some of the *Umbra* poems of Pound. There are to be found, for example, Yeatsian celtic images and echoes of verbal effects, especially in some of the poems written in 1908. The poem *La Frainsne* published in *A Lume Spento*, 1908 shows Yeats's influence. Some other poems, too, echo Yeats's themes, language and imaginative world. *Anima Sola* is an example. The poem *La Fraisne* presents a natural world which recalls the world of Yeats's *In the Seven Woods*. The view of nature as a great refuge to the suffering humanity is common to both Yeats's poem and *La Fraisne* of Pound.[24] In addition to casual echoes of W.B. Yeats, *La Fraisne* presents natural beauty and its soothing effects on the restless mind of the protagonist.

La Fraisne deals with an invented character Miraut de Garzelas. The plot of the poem bristles with metaphysical value of society and spirit. Pound wrote a note to this poem and kept it till 1920. Although the poem presents Yeatsian moods, Pound refers to a passage in *Janus of Basel* in his note to the poem:

> When the soul is exhausted of fire, then doth the spirit return unto its primal nature and there is upon it a peace great and of the woodland
>
> *"magna pax et silvestris."*
>
> Then becometh it kin to the faun and the dryad, a woodland-dweller amid the rocks and streams
>
> *"consociis faunis dryadisque-inter sexa sylvarum."*[25]

The note of Pound further mentions the natural world of W.B. Yeats which deals with the woodland and ethereal beauty. In addition, it refers to Father Sinistrari's treatise *Daemonalitas*. Pound's main concern becomes clear: the presentation of natural beauty and the mysterious experience of life with peace. Pound refers to Yeats's *Celtic Twilight*. The method adopted helps sincere expression. He presents a wide world of the Universe which consists of the tree, pool, spirit, God and natural attendants evoking a mystical perspective. The assumed legendary story of Miraut de Garzelas enables Pound to fuse the experiences of Lai de Fraisne of Marie del France with La Frainse. The experience of La Fraisne becomes the very similitudes of that of Miraut de Garzelas, Piere Vidal, etc. The theme of love unifies them, lit up with the love of women 'that plague and burn and drive one away."

In *La Fraisne* the speaker presents his experience of his old age as well as his youth. He narrates his suffering, happiness, bitterness and identifies his lady with Nature:

> Because my bride
> Is a pool of the wood, and
> Though all men say that I am mad
> It is only that I am glad,

Very glad, for my bride hath toward me a great love
That is sweeter than the lover of women
That plague and burn and drive one away.

(*EPSP*, p. 33)

The speaker of the poem suffers from madness resembling the insanity of Piere Vidal who ran after Na Loba. The poem's theme is also related to that of *The Madness of King Goll* (1889)[26] written by W.B. Yeats. The speaker describes his mental agony as experienced by him. The poet presents the mood and psychic experience of the character who became a tree. Pound finds metamorphosis in natural things. The aetheral soul can find happiness by marrying a wood. The love of nature and passion for the woman are brought in contrast, which makes distinction between a real and an imaginative world. Nature provides relief and peace to the suffering protagonist.

The narrator remembers his past days which present his follies and meaningless wisdom. He had been a councillor and in his youth was full of strength. The word "Sword-play" shows the strength of physical potency which attracts a woman, for she values chivalry. The next two stanzas deal with the mood of the speaker. The transformation makes it possible to love the "ash wood," "still pool," and "dog-wood."

The poem brings many conclusions. It takes an ethical turn: human beings should live a life of love as spirits and objects of nature. They have a harmonious living of their own. Allegorically, the spirits are like human-beings constituting their own community, full of life-force and universal vitality. The natural surroundings (with tree, water, pool, dogwood and air) symbolically interpret different values. Water, tree, and leaves form the idea of sustenance which stimulates other things of the nature. The wind that "flutters in the leaves" represents the force of the nature.

The poem presents an ecstasy. The natural world of spirits and soul presents the fantasy of the mystical nature. Later on, this celtic world also appears in his Chinese poems. But the portrayal of nature belongs to the tradition of Provence. In this poem, the setting comes from Yeatsian world, but the note of Pound also mentions Piere Vidal's madness. The reference of forest presents the world of nature. The nature of Provencal poetry presents an equation: in "most Provencal poetry one finds nature in its proper place, i.e. as a background to the action, an interpretation of the mood; an equation, in other terms, or a 'metaphor by sympathy' for the mood of the poem."[27]

There are obvious parallels in Pound's and Yeat's poems. The speakers in both *La Fraisne* and *In the Seven Woods* want to escape the suffering of madness. But Pound's speaker presents a wider world of experience, and his poem is written in a conversational form. The persona shows his growth. He is seen developing from youth to age. In the second part of the poem there are elliptical remarks and discontinuous rhythm. In the first three stanzas there is metrical brilliance and rhythmic spontaneity. The rhyming,scheme is ab ab; there are also initial rhymes. Similarly, the second and the third stanzas adopt the same basic metrical pattern with varying off-beat rhymes in the last stanza. The first stanza has assonance; the poet deliberately uses similar vowels in stressed words such as gaunt, councillor, wise, old, aside, folly, cold, and cloak. The rhyme places "additional emphasis upon the already ambiguous nature of an ostensible run-on line ending. The first connection of cold is accomplished by means of rhyme. The other connection is established, of course, by the syntax, but also by the placement of cold and cloak in successive line-ending positions"[28] which stresses the mild paradox of statement.

The articulating sound of the first stanza is continued in the next three stanzas as the poet uses such words as sword, folly, more, boles, wood, oak, yoke, cast, aside. But the poem takes an abrupt turn, and the repetition of the sentences "I have put aside" in the second and fifth stanzas brings a sharp contrast between things. The rhyming pattern changes from stanza to stanza as the move of the poet undergoes change. Pound's poems, in general, show a flexible adaptability of metre to mood. The /a/ and /o/ vowel sounds reinforce the sense of grief of the speaker:

I wrapped my tears in an ellum leaf
And left them under a stone
And now men call me mad because I have thrown
All folly from me, putting it aside
To leave the old barren ways of men,

(*EPSP*, p. 33)

The lines just cited are marked by simplicity and contemporaneity of vocabulary.

La Fraisne has a medieval correlation of imagery, theme, and metamorphic suggestions. But what Pound communicates to his contemporaries is a double vision of human realities that have existed since the human history began and that still exist. There is a negative vision of human society which is pervaded by vanity, and consequent frustration. The frustrating vanity of women, vanity of swordsmen, and rancorous vanity of councillors are the actualities of human society which bring madness. The poem also evokes a positive vision of a life inspired by love.

In Durance presents a world of aesthetic tradition and artistic creativity. The title echoing Samuel Butler's *Hudibras*, is suggestive of imprisonment in which the Poet lives, a surrounding of "friendly faces" unlike his kith and kins. The concept of "imprisonment" has my suggestions which point out the mental isolation and seclusion of the speaker. The poem presents the experience of exile. It deals with the period when Pound was held up in the Middle West.[29] Because of unfavourable circumstances, a kind of hollowness existed in the literary world; it checked the growth of healthy traditions. After the publication of *A Lume Spento* (1908), when Pound appeared on the scene of London and joined the circle of contemporary poets, he felt free. In his poem *The Rest* he says that he is no longer in durance. This poem belongs to a group of poems such as *The Decadence, Grace before Song, Masks*, and *L'Art*, which present the personal point of view of life and art. *In Durance* looks into "the past in search of artists who were faced with the same difficulties as he is, and, by quotations, brings their experience to bear upon us."[30]

The poem begins with the date 1907, when Pound stayed in Indiana and suffered from mental suffocation in an atmosphere of artistic stagnation. In one of his letters addressed to William Carlos Williams, in 1908, Pound states his bitter experience. Pound suffered from defamation because he fed a hungry woman and gave her shelter. Although the letter does not narrate the incident, it indirectly hints at the behaviour of the people of Indiana.[31] The poem begins in a conversational tone:

> I am homesick after mine own kind,
> Oh I know that there are folk about, friendly-faces,
> But I am homesick after mine own kind.
>
> (*EPSP*, p. 47)

The speaker expresses his feeling of suffering and asks his fellow artists to be with him. He feels uncommunicative to ordinary people who are friendly, but callous and indifferent to poets and writers. Moreover, the speaker deals with the low mentality of the middle class society in which art is totally debased. His fellow writers in his "prison," are commercial-minded. The second stanza expresses the bitterness:

> 'These sell our pictures'! Oh well,
> They reach me not, touch me some edge or that,
> But reach me not and all my life's become
> One flame, that reaches not beyond
>
> (*EPSP*, p. 47)

The first line is a quotation and comes from *Pictor Ignotus* by Browning. "These buy and sell our pictures, take and give,/ Count them for garniture and household-stuff."[32] Browning also presents the mental makeup of the reading public. The repetition of "I am homesick" makes for emphasis. The persona uses it several times in the poem which reinforces the emphatic tone. He feels homesick because he finds himself in a hostile situation for art. He also suffers from a lack of recognition.

In Durance, expresses the disgust and disappointment of the speaker. The contemporary neglect of artistic works is due to the commercial motive of selling and buying. These are offered to the Poet as possible inspiration. The speaker, not finding a proper response, feels "in durance." The surrounding is one of the dampness of imprisoned, suffocated, dejected life; it is contrasted with the beauty and grandeur of hills and sea, which become the real dwelling place of the kith and kins of the protagonist. The speaker attacks the taste of the Georgian period and the literary circle of England in 1920. The poetic mode of T.S. Eliot and Ezra Pound met with opposition. The poem seems to be prophetic in tone, as it underlines the condemnation of the taste of the literary audience of the time when the poem was written. A poet could not find any stimulus in his cultural environment. If the Chinese, the Provencal, the Greek, the Italians, and the Medieval poets had not offered Pound a spiritual stimulus, his poetic fires might have smouldered away without having been awakened to a creative glow for lack of a responsive audience.

The poem rises above the personal and autobiographical details. Thematically, it condemns "Philistinism" of the age. It also studies the painful victimization of "outcasts." If the poem is important for artistic aspirations, inherent aesthetic values, and theoretical pronouncements, it is equally important for its demonstration of technical form. The poem indirectly echoes Whitman's view of art and artists. *Pax Saturn* and *Commission* also deal with opposition to the arts in hostile situations. The tone of the speaker expresses his plight: "Oh I know, Oh well, Oh ye." Pound expresses a similar disgust in *The Rest* and *The Flame*. In the first poem the few artists that there are, are shown "broken," "mistrusted," "starved," and "helpless." *The Flame* presents a flock of ordinary men and women who do not have any response to the transcendental beauty.

The major images in *In Durance* are hills, seas, sun, trees, birds, fire and home. These suggest a desirable state of affairs. The quotations and allusions are used as a poetic device which presents universal significance to "a personal statement or emotion."[33] The allusion to Butler's poem *Hudibras* is intended to underline the mental agony of the speaker. The reference to Browning shows the decline of taste for art. The reference of Coleridge dealing with "Quasi Kaloun" suggests the sublime beauty. With these allusions of contrasting tenor, Pound makes the setting evocative. The poem shows the involvement and detachment of the poet in different contexts. The metaphor of heart and hearth, soul-kin, life as "one flame," "I love ye" as the wind, the tree" are interpretative. The actualities of devalued social milieu mingle with facts of the sublime concept of beauty. The poem presents the experience of an artist who is an outcast.

Pound's method of excernment presents the best traditions of the Provencal, Italian, German, and French poetry. Pound studied the literature and culture of the twelfth century Provence. The Provencal poets, especially the Tuscan, experimented several forms of verse which still seem to be relevant and useful. Pound also shows interest in Arnaut Daniel, Guido Cavalcanti, and Dante for their technical brilliance and presentation of objects. Pound's *Marvoil, Piere Vidal Old, Sestina: Altaforte,* and *Na Audiart* present the themes of the Troubadours: their masks deal with the ethics of love and war. Pound translated about fifty poems from the Provencal poetry during 1908-1910. In these translations he has practised the use of English for expressing the emotion and cult of the Provencal poets; and to a great extent, he is successful in his efforts. His translations mean a mode of composition. Most of the Provencal poets are warriors, jongleurs and lovers who sing in the context of the social and political setup of their time. Guillaume, Count of Peiteus, wrote songs. His wife, Countess of Dia, fell in love with Rainbaut d'Aurenga. Bertran de Born was a poet and warrior. Rudel, Arnaut Daniel and Vidal were also great singers of their time. The songs of the poets and jongleurs, who were mostly singers, deal with the contemporary theme of love, intrigue and warfare. These poets and their songs tell us about the natural beauty of mountains to serve a point of contrast to fashion and modes of contemporary Provencal life. The

Provencal poets not only give us romance and decorative art but are also relevant to our social values.[34]

Na Audiart, Marvoil, and *Piere Vidal Old* ha\ the protagonists which are the poet's personae; they express the ıdventures and poetic craftsmanship of their creators. *Planh for t e Young English King* presents the story of Prince Henry Plantagenet, the eldest son of Henry II, who fought against his father and, later, died of illness. The poem is a lament written by Bertran de Born. These poems deal with the cult and emotions of an important tradition.

The poem *Na Audiart* deals with the love story of a Provencal poet, Bertran de Born. He is famous as the lover of the lady Maent of Montaignac and a poet of war. *Na Audiart* is an expression of vanity, fading physical beauty, and faithless love. Bertran de Born was dismissed by the lady from her court. Born wrote a poem in her praise and made many efforts to win her favour. Pound writes in a note:

> Anyone who has read anything of the Troubadours knows well the tale of Bertran de Born and My Lady Maent of Montaignac, and knows also the song he made when she would none of him, the song wherein he, seeking to find or make her equal, begs of each preeminent lady of Langue d'Oc some trait or some fair semblance: thus of Cembelins her 'esgart amoros' to wit, her love-lit glance, of Aelis her speech free-running, of the Vicomtess of Chalais her throat and her two hands, at Roacoart of Anhes her hair golden as Iseult's: and even in this fashion of Lady Audiart 'although she would that ill come unto him' he sought and praised the lineaments of the torse.[35]

Bertran de Born is the speaker of this poem. Pound introduces him as a lover. The poem begins with his heartfelt feelings of love; he praises her beauty:

> Though thou well dost wish me ill,
> Audiart, Audiart,
> Where thy bodice laces start
> As ivy fingers clutching through
> Its crevices,
> Audiart, Audiart,
> Stately, tall and lovely tender

Who shall render
                    Audiart, Audiart,
Praises meet unto thy fashion?
Here a word kiss!

(*EPSP*, p. 36)

The protagonist has used the name of the lady, Audiart, several times, five times to be exact. The repetition emphasizes and expresses the tone of the speaker. The first address expresses the anguish of the speaker, because the lady thinks ill of him. The second address expresses his awareness of the beauty of the lady. The same theme is repeated by Pound in the latter part of the poem. The poem has been written in an unconventional metrical pattern, with irregular length of lines. The persona presents his mental agony, sadness, and isolation. His sadness alternates with his lovely and is growing old with wrinkled face and old soul.

The growing age of the lady and the growing sadness are presented effectively. The speaker reminds the lady and her fading beauty:

Youth dew is cold
Upon thy hands, and thy old soul
Scorning a new, wry'd casement,...

(*EPSP*, p. 37)

This contrasts with the warmth and charm of youth. The tone of the speaker becomes emphatic. The poem is, thematically, a "blending of fixed feelings of satire, pity, pride, praise, rejection and lust, that find expression with suitable words and phrases of ostensible enjambment."[36] The beauty presented by *Na Audiart* is platonic, even though the speaker presents sensuous details such as "girdle's scope" and "torse and limbs." The decaying beauty makes the lady aware of the cruelty of time. The poet suggests that his art can preserve her beauty in his verses.

Piere Vidal Old deals with the theme of love. Piere Vidal, a poet, is presented as a lover. He loved Na Loba and, in the appreciation of her beauty, wrote several songs. The character of Vidal in this poem is a mixture of reality and fiction. The background of the poem belongs to the legend of Vidal. Pound mentions in a note the details of Vidal's love:

> It is of Peire Vidal, the fool *par excellence* of all Provence, of whom the tale tells how he ran mad, as a wolf, because of his love for Loba of Penautier, and how men hunted him with dogs through the mountains of Cabaret and brought him for dead to the dwelling of this Loba (she-wolf) of Penautier, and how she and her Lord had him healed and made welcome, and he stayed some time at that court.[37]

The note of Pound gives a clue to the poem. The theme is concerned with the psychological perversion of a man whose passion leads him to the extent of insanity. This suggests a kind of animal passion or "dipsomania."[38] Pound borrowed the idea of madness of Vidal's poem *Vida,* "though you call me a wolf, I do not feel that I am dishonoured." Pound also makes Vidal undergo a metamorphosis. He is turned into a wolf. The transformation of human beings into animals or natural objects is also to be found in *La Fraisne,* in which the protagonist establishes his relationship with non-human objects. The poem contains eleven strophes. In the first strophe he appears as a persona of Piere Vidal who had, in his past life, suffered from madness. The speaker recapitulates his past tragic experience:

> When I but think upon the great dead days
> And turn my mind upon that splendid madness,
> Lo! I do curse my strength
> And blame the sun his gladness;
> For that the one is dead
> And the red sun mocks my sadness.
>
> (*EPSP*, p. 55)

The second stanza is about the physical strength and ability of the speaker. He feels proud of the songs which were sung by other jongleurs of his time. The third stanza deals with his madness in making attempts to see his lady naked. He was enamoured of her beauty—her "purpling lips," "thin silk stuff" and "white body." The tone changes, and he speaks to Vidal and calls him a "fool of fools." He expresses his mental involvement with physical attraction of the lady. He feels dumbfounded:

> . Speech? Words? Faugh ! who talks of words and love?!
> Hot is such love and silent,
> Silent as fate is, and as strong until
> It faints in taking and in giving all.
>
> (*EPSP*, p. 56)

The psssion of love cannot endure for a long time. The poem ends with a positive vision which makes the speaker to realize the worth of his songs and poems.

The speaker in *Planh for the Young English King* is the mask of Bertran de Born. At the funeral of the Young English King, Bertran wrote his poem in decasyllabic verse, with a rhyme scheme of Abab CddE. The first and the last word of each stanza in original Provencal poem produced sound effect which underscores the mournful tone of the lament.[39]

Sestina: Altaforte deals with the experience of a warrior. The poem is, again, concerned with the story of Bertran de Born who appears as a "stirrer of strife," as described by Dante. Pound also experiments with the form of Sestina on which he worked in the British Museum. The *Sestina* is developed by Pound on the model of Arnaut Daniel. In it the most predominant quality is its musical and rhythmic display of words. The form of Sestina was introduced in Italy by Dante and in Spain by Fernado de Herrera. The form is like a "thin sheet of flame folding and unfolding."[40] Pound deals with theme as well as form of his models.

The story of Bertran de Born as a warrior is very interesting. He instigated brothers to fight against brothers. The English King Henry fought against his brother Richard, because Bertran de Born enticed him to do so in 1170. Dante, for Born's lust of war, put him in the 8th circle of his inferno and Pound treats him in the like manner in his *Hell Cantos*. The technical form of the poem provides Pound with the idea of action. The poem is a translation and an example of "criticism in new composition."[41]

The poem begins with an epigraph which reveals the punishment of the speaker in Dante. The poem contains seven stanzas. The opening lines begin in a conversational tone:

> Damn it all ! all this our South stinks peace.
>
> You whoreson dog, Papiols, come ! Let's to music!
>
> I have no life save when the swords clash.
>
> But ah ! When I see the standards gold , vair, purple, opposing
>
> And the broad fields beneath them turn crimson, Then howl
> I my heart nigh mad with rejoicing.
>
> (*EPSP*, p. 53)

The first two lines show the spirit of the protagonist. The speaker of the poem seeks pleasure in banners, swords, and fields flooded with blood. The war spirit of the protagonist finds enjoyment in the rising sun that spreads its crimson colour on the horizon. The poet presents images of "blood crimson," "spears," "dark clash" and swords, which present the atmosphere of war. Born is Pound's ironic persona. Indirectly, the poem is a satire on war mongers. Born becomes a type of war mongers of all times and all places.

Both a vision of human strife and a vision of nature's strife are vividly rendered in the poem. The protagonist visualizes the southern Europe as troubled with tempest in summer, and the sky rent with lightning and thunder. He can enjoy nature in its violent moods as a background to violent human action.

In the Sestina from of the poem, there is a repetition of the last words in each line. It consists of six verses with a final triplet. The form has been used by Spenser, Swinburne, Sidney, and W.H. Auden. It consists of six stanzas in each of which there are six lines and an envoy. Usually the lines are unrhymed but the repetition takes place of rhyme in the final words which occur in the following order:

Stanza 1 A B C D E F

2 F A E B D C

3 C F D A B E

4 E C B F A D

5 D E A C F B

6 B D F E C A

Envoy B D F or A C E.[42]

Often the envoy uses all the final words, 2 to a line:

B E; D C; F A, as invented by Arnaut Daniel.

This form with six rhyme-words and a constant recurrence of musical beats can express intense feelings and emotions in a lyrical poem. But according to Christoph de Nagy, the form is an unsuitable vehicle of coherent thought.[43] The first stanza is an example of free verse closer to speech rhythm. The words, peace, music, clash, opposing, crimson and rejoicing, make the order in which words occur at the end of the lines in the first stanza. The pattern of the first stanza is retained in the second and third stanzas, too. In the second stanza, the first line ends with the end-word of the last line of the first stanza, and the second line with the end-word of the first; the third line with that of the fifth; fourth with that of the second; fifth with that of fourth; and the sixth with that of the third.

The third stanza is linked, in the like manner, to the second; the fourth to the third; the fifth to the fourth; the sixth to the fifth; and the seventh stanza, constituting the *Envoy* of the poem, repeats the end words of the second half of the sixth stanza in the same order, ECA. That is, the first line of the Envoy ends with the last word of the fourth line of sixth stanza, second line with that of the fifth, the third with that of the sixth line of the sixth stanza. Pound has brought some changes in the form of Sestina in stanza four as he has interchanged the end-words of the third and the fourth lines; and the pattern of Pound's envoy is a repetition of the pattern of the last three lines in the sixth stanza. T.S. Eliot considers this poem the "best Sestina that has been written in English."[44]

Pound revolted against the conventional prosody of Browning, the Pre-Raphaelites, and other nineteenth century poets in order to bring the rhythm of poetry close to the rhythm of actual speech, with the result that is not possible to scan his

Sestina according to the conventional prosody. The poem begins with speech rhythm "Damn it all! All this our South stinks peace/ You whoreson dog Papiols, come! Let's to music !" But in the second stanza it approaches some regularity and pattern in the syllabic length of the time. This tension between fixity and flux is confined, in this poem only to syllabic length of time. But in order to overcome the defects of speech rhythm Pound has used the intricate pattern of the six words terminating lines that gives the poem a formal pattern, which goes well with the way in which the poem's theme unfolds itself, in a repetitive manner.

Pound's study of the Tuscan poetry presents the art and emotion of its cult. The Tuscan poets, such as Arnaut Daniel and Guido Cavalcanti, manifest a lyrical tradition of medieval poetry. Arnaut Daniel was a very popular singer and a song writer. Pound's discussion of Daniel appears in his critical works, e.g. *The Spirit of Romance* (1910) and *Instigations* (1920).

Pound shows his interest in Canzoni, which, in Provencal poetry, is known as Canzon and as Canzone in Italy. The poem is popular for its music which appeals even to modern readers and is found very close to Roman and Hellenic music.[45] Arnaut Daniel's Canzone is famous for its sound and rhyme. He uses a different number of rhymes in each song, in which words are used as musical notes. Arnaut Daniel gives an aesthetic of sound and presents opaque and clear sounds with obvious distinctions.[46]

Pound has translated a number of Canzones, in which he tries to render the sensibility and emotion of his models. *Exultations* (1909) contained five Canzons:

> *The Yearly Slain. The Vision, The Spear, To be Sung Beneath a Window* and *Of Incense* in which Pound presents the theme of love; and the woman appears as an ideal lady who possesses beauty and virtues. In *The Yearly Slain*, Pound presents Kore as endowed with matchless beauty; and *The Vision* presents a mystic world which is suffused with ecstasy. *The Spear* expresses the anguish and pain of a lover. When Pound

> presented these poems to Ford Madox Ford, who had published four of Canzoni, he showed his dislike for them, because the poems demonstrated only polish and refinement of British poetry written from 1890 to 1910. But Pound continued to work on Provencal poetry, especially on Daniel's poems, as they propounded a technique of sound.[47]

In the Canzon *The House of Splendour* the speaker presents the power of love. The theme of the poem is based on the story of II Corinthians and Pater's story of the "Cupid and Psyche" in *Marius the Epicurean.*[48] The story of psyche and cupid presents a beautiful world of trees, flowers, bushes and nature's serenity. The poem begins with the description of a house which is supposed to be the house of the beloved of the protagonist of the poem. The house represents the virtues of the lady, who illuminates the environment with her golden appearance. As the house is analogous to the beauty and virtues of the lady, the walls of the house are carved out in golden paintings. The images of sun, sapphires, pale, gold, claret stone, aureate light and email evoke the vision of a magical and energetic form of the woman. The house and the woman are adored by the speaker:

> Here am I come perforce my love of her,
> Behold mine adoration
> Maketh me clear, and there are powers in this
> Which, played on by the virtues of her soul,
> Break down the four-square walls of standing time.
>
> (*EPSP*, p. 67)

The Flame expresses the isolation of the poet-artist. The speaker of the poem faces a hostile situation which opposes real art. The flame is a metaphor for the artist's inspiration. The narrator of the poem uses "we" to speak for the entire class of poets and artists. He praises province for its beauty, ethics, tales, manner and ecstasy of love, which supply enough content to poets: "We of the Ever-living, in that light/Meet through our veils and whisper, and of love". The repetition of "Tis not a game" four times in the poem reinforces the mood. The protagonist presents two situations represented by "we" and "you," the artist and his society. The hostility between these two is manifested in the mood of the poem. In the last part of the poem, the narrator shifts from "we" to "I".

Pound also translated some of the Ballate of Guido Cavalcanti, who occupies a very important place in Tuscan poetry. Pound has translated Cavalcanti's *Bonna Mi Prega,* in which the poet presents the image of perfect love. A ballate is made up of a folk-song for dance. The ballate song produces musical effects because of its rhythm, and it deals with the theme of love that is more emotional than the Italian Canzone.[49] The ballate deals with the theme of love which is a common point between the lover and the woman. The lady is presented as an ideal woman. Guido himself was a superb poet. His poetry, in general, presents many qualities:

> Than Guido Cavalcanti no psychologist of the emotions is more keen in his understanding, more precise in his expression, we have in him no rhetoric, but always a true description, whether it be of pain itself, or of the apathy that comes when the emotions and possibilities of emotion are exhausted, or of that stranger state when the feeling by its intensity surpasses our powers of bearing and we seem to stand aside and watch it surging across some thing or being with whom we are no longer identified.[50]

The subtle psychological understanding of the emotion, precise presentation, and non-rhetorical use of language are the great characteristics of Cavalcanti's poetic craftsmanship. *Umbra* (1920) contains ballates II-III, V-VII, and XI-XIV. In these ballates, Cavalcanti presents the ethics of love, beauty of the woman, and the experience of the lover. Ballata II opens with the vision of a lady:

> Fair women I saw passing where she passed;
>
> And none among them women, to my vision;
>
> But were like nothing save her shadow cast.[51]

The last four lines of Ballata II express the agony of the speaker's mind on the thought of death. The speaker makes a pronouncement of his death which fills the heart of the protagonist with memories of the lady. Pound translated the lines just quoted from the following:

> Io vidi donne con la donna mia:
> Non cbe niuna mi sembrasse donna;
> Ma simiglivan sol la sua ombria.[52]

The sound and cadence of "mia," "donna," and "ombria," have been rendered by Pound as "passed," "vision," and "cast." The sound effect found in the sentence "Vidi donne con la donna mia" has been rendered with exactness in "Fair women I saw passing where she passed." The precise words convey the emotion of the sufferer who fears to lose his beloved. The poet tries his best to capture the moment of emotional intensity, which is rendered in "Cruel. ... For sobbing out my heart's full memories."

Apart from these poems, Pound has also translated several poems from other European languages. His translations and adaptations from Heine were published in *Canzoni of Ezra Pound* (1911). He reprinted only the eighth poem from Heine in *Umbra* (1920). Pound's interest in Heine was for his lyric and tricky use of words. He makes only casual remarks on the poetry of Heine. In German literature there was a revolt against postivitism during 1900-1920. The writers and poets of Germany changed the old tradition of their literature with new ideas and new forms. The typological form of literature was presented with new trends. Heine was known as "Nazarener and Hellener, as Matthew Arnold."[53] The VIIIth translation from Heine is entitled *Night Song*:

> And have you thoroughly kissed my lips?
> There was no particular haste,
> And are you not ready when evening's come?
> There's no *particular* haste.
> You've got the whole night before you,
> Heart's-all-beloved-my-own;
> In an uninterrupted night one can
> Get a good deal of kissing done.[54]

The poem contains two stanzas of four lines each. In the first stanza, the second line—"There's no particular haste"—has been repeated as the fourth line. The speaker advises the lover not to make haste and wait till night. The first line is interrogative. The second line refers to the kissing already done. But the speaker suggests to her lover not to become impatient "as there's no particular haste."

Umbra reprints more than a dozen poems from *Ripostes* (1912), dealing with different themes; such as paganism, mythic transformation, city, urbanity and medieval beauty. *Pan is Dead, Surgit Famma* and *The Return* present pagan gods and goddesses. *A Girl* is concerned with the explication of a delightful psychic experience. *The Seafarer* is a translation of the famous Anglo-Saxon poem.

Some of the poems of *Umbra* (1920)—*Portrait d'une Femme, The Return* and *The Seafarer*— are remarkable for their use of modern language and Pound's contemporary sensibility. Even the poem *Silet,* which is like a sonnet, is written in modern language. *The Tomb at Akr Caar* is written in the form of a monologue; but *A Virginal, Sub Mare,* and *The Needle* are set in the medieval world. These poems have "withstood fifty years of changing fashions in verse, and have had, in addition, a profound influence on the practitioners who count."[55]

Portrait d'une Femme expresses a contemporary theme and posits Pound's criticism on London. It presents the portrait of a woman whose identity has been lost because of her involvement with ideas and the intellectual setup of London. The protagonist of the poem reminds the lady of her position; her physical appearance and mental rottenness seem to be the "Sargasso Sea":

> Your mind and you are our Sargasso Sea,
> London has swept about you this score years
> And bright ships left you this or that in fee:
> Ideas, old gossip, oddments of all things,
> Strange spars of knowledge and dimmed wares of price.

(*EPSP*, p. 74)

The lady has completely lost her identity, and also her native virtues. Unlike the ladies of the Canzones, the woman portrayed has no radiance, no magnetism and no refinement. She is always secondary. The tone of the speaker is ironical, for the character of the woman is observed and criticized from outside. Her trivial, shallow and hollow personality is exposed. She appears a lifeless, virtuless, and charmless woman. She appears to be nothing herself:

> No! there is nothing! In the whole and all,
> Nothing that's quite your own.
> Yet this is you.
>
> (*EPSP*, p. 75)

A Girl expresses a sad psychic experience which belongs to a mythical world:

> The tree has entered my hands,
> The sap has ascended my arms,
> The tree has grown in my breast—
> Downward,
> The branches grow out of me, like arms.
>
> (*EPSP*, p. 75)

The poem recalls the stories of Apollo and Daphne and of Philemon and Baucis in Ovid's *Metamorphoses* (I and VIII). Philemon and Baucis became trees after their death. Daphne and Apollo present the theme of love and passion that amounted to rape. In order to save herself from Apollo's effort at seduction, Daphne became a tree. The poem is an evocation of a mood. The mythic experience of the girl is rendered by means of equations of natural objects. Tree, sap, branches, moss etc. present the experience of a vegetable world. Pound has defined poetry as a presentation of equations of emotions. In this context his definition of poetry is worth mentioning: "Poetry is a sort of inspired mathematics, which gives us equations, not for abstract figures, triangles, spheres, and the like, but equations for the human emotions."[56]

The Return presents the experience of an objective reality. The poem deals with pagan gods, who also appear in *Surgit*

Fama and *Pan is Dead.* Pound showed a keen interest in paganism. The first line is a dramatic presentation of ideas. The poet makes gods and goddesses appear in the world. Their appearance with feelings of fear has been presented objectively. The speaker is, again, confronted with a hostile situation, which is represented with Christian values. The poem begins on a conversational note:

> See, they return; ah, see the tentative
> Movements, and the slow feet,
> The trouble in the pace and the uncertain
> Wavering!

(*EPSP*, p. 85)

The poem can be divided into three parts. The first part deals with the entrance of gods who move with "slow feet." The second part, again, points to the gods coming slowly. The poet presents the movements of gods through the images "snow," and "murmur in the wind," which denote the disturbance in the atmosphere. He also suggests the reaction of the Christian world, which does not like paganism at all. Christians have been presented as "silver hounds." The word "see" is used three times, "they return" two times, "Winged" two times. These are the elements of repetition. There is no vagueness and ambiguity in the poem, which presents the return of gods with sharp and clear images.

The Seafarer is a free translation of the old English poem. The main purpose of the composition of this poem was to invent a language to produce appropriate sound and rhythm. The purpose was not to avoid variations in rendering the literal sense. Pound's version is important for the exact rendering of the rhythm in modern language. The translation of the poem first appeared in *New Age* in 1912 with a heading *The New Method of Literary Scholarship*. The poem presents the theme of quest, the protagonist narrates his experience of journey. The poem renders the self-analysis of the persona who confronts men who belong to different social standards. Several of the images used suggest the nature of the hardships and obstacles faced by the adventurer.

The Anglo-Saxon verse has accentual metre. Each verse line has four main stresses and the poet can use as many weak syllables between the stresses as he needs. The first half-line is linked to the second half-line by means of alliteration. Pound departs from the rigid pattern to suit the demands of modern speech:

> Pound breaks the rules and constantly uses the forbidden half-lines, in which the two lifts come together and the two dips merge, did produce, by way of error, what was to become the characteristic Poundian line, ending in either a spondee (two stressed syllables together), or, on the contrary, in several unaccented syllables (i.e. the last two forbidden half-lines above: xxx...and...xxxx).[57]

The "characteristic Poundian line" was not invented out of error, but was an act of deliberate choice. Pound uses alliteration when it comes handy: "Journey's jargon," "Bitter-breast," "Narrow night watch nigh," "May make merry man," "Neareth night shade," "fronts frost," and "Cuckoo calleth."

The poems of *Umbra* (1920) discussed in the preceding pages are characterized by modern diction, subtle rhythm, and apt images. They contain intensity of thought and emotion, which mark the modern sensibility of the maturing Ezra Pound. They present the cult of emotion, the cult of culture, and poetic craftsmanship of a conscious artist. The study of the early poems which Pound wanted to keep in circulation in 1920s are his earnest efforts in the search for an adequate language and idiom. His translations and adaptations have enriched English poetry with several traditions of Southern European languages. These poems demonstrate the art of technical excellence and use of personae as a literary device. Pound's poems, thus, belong to the method of excernment which presents the best examples of poets who help to make new compositions. His early involvement with Tuscan and Provencal poets and modern conditions helps him mature as a modern poet.

REFERENCES

1. Christine Brooke-Rose, *A ZBC of Ezra Pound* (London: Faber and Faber, 19710), p. 79.

2. Eric Homberger, ed., "Introduction", *The Critical Heritage* (London: Routledge and Kegan Paul, 1972), p. 6.
3. F.S. Flint, *New Age* (27 May 1909), pp. 101-02.
4. Edward Thomas, "Two Poets", *English Review II, (June 1909),* pp. *627-28.*
5. F.S. Flint, "Verse," *New Age,* VI (6 Jan. 1910), 233-34.
6. Edwin Muir, "Review", *Umbra; The Early Poems of Ezra Pound, New Age,* 22 July, 1920, xxvii, pp. 186-87.
7. N. Christoph de Nagy, *The Poetry of Ezra Pound: The Pre-Imagist Stage* (Bern: Francke Verlag, 1960), p. 53.
8. T.S. Eliot, ed., "Introduction", *Ezra Pound: Selected Poems* (London: Faber and Faber, 1928), p. 3.
9. *Literary Essays of Ezra Pound,* ed. T.S. Eliot, (London: Faber and Faber, 1968), p. 371.
10. Herbert N. Schneidau, *Ezra Pound: The Image and the Real* (Baton Rogue: Louisiana State University Press, 1969), p. 26.
11. Ezra Pound, *The Spirit of Romance* (London: Peter Owen, 1910), p. 87.
12. *Ibid.*, p. 223.
13. K.K. Ruthven, "Introduction," *A Guide to Ezra Pound's Personae, 1926* (Berkeley and Los Angeles: University of California Press, 1969), p. 4.
14. Ezra Pound, "Vorticism," *Fortnightly Review,* XCVII, 573 (Sept., 1, 1914), pp. 463-64.
15. D.D. Paige, ed., *The Selected Letters of Ezra Pound* (London: Faber and Faber, 1971), p. 8.
16. Monroe K. Spears, *Dionysus and the City* (London: Oxford University Press, 1970), p. 41.
17. Quoted in Hugh Witemeyer, *The Poetry of Ezra Pound: Forms and Renewal 1908-20* (Berkeley and Los Angeles: University of California Press, 1969), p. 49.
18. *The Selected Letters of Ezra Pound,* pp. 3-4.
19. *Ezra Pound: Selected Poems,* ed. T.S. Eliot (London: Faber and Faber, 1928), p. 34. This source will be abbreviated to EPSP and references to it will be made in the body of the text.
20. K.K. Ruthven, *A Guide to Ezra Pound's Personae* (1926), p. 50.
21. Thomas H. Jackson, *The Early Poetry of Ezra Pound* (Cambridge, Mass.: Harvard University Press, 1968), pp. 120-21.
22. N. Christoph de Nagy, "Pound and Browning", *New Approaches to Ezra Pound,* ed., Eva Hesse (London: Faber and Faber, 1969), p. 90.

23. *Ibid.*, pp. 105-07.
24. Thomas H. Jackson, *The Early Poetry of Ezra Pound*, pp. 130-31.
25. Quoted in K.K. Ruthven, *A Guide to Ezra Pound's Personae*, 1926, pp. 158-59.
26. Hugh Witemeyer, *The Poetry of Ezra Pound: Forms and Renewal, 1908-20* (Berkeley: University of California Press, 1969), p. 63.
27. Ezra Pound, *The Spirit of Romance*, p. 31.
28. Thomas H. Jackson, *The Early Poetry of Ezra Pound*, p. 133.
29. K.K. Ruthven, *A Guide to Ezra Pound's Personae*, 1926, p. 154.
30. N. Christoph de Nagy, *The Poetry of Ezra Pound: The Pre-Imagist Stage* (Bern: Francke Verlag, 1968), pp. 27-28.
31. D.D. Paige, ed. *Selected Letters of Ezra Pound*, p. 5.
32. Quoted in K.K. Ruthven, *A Guide to Ezra Pound's Personae*, 1926, p. 154.
33. N. Christoph de Nagy, *The Poetry of Ezra Pound: The Pre-Imagist Stage*, p. 43.
34. *Literary Essays of Ezra Pound*, pp. 94-101.
35. *Ezra Pound: Selected Poems*, p. 36.
36. Thomas H. Jackson, *The Early Poetry of Ezra Pound*, pp. 136-37.
37. *Selected Poems of Ezra Pound*, p. 55.
38. K.K. Ruthven, *A Guide to Ezra Pound's Personae*, 1926, p. 194.
39. Stuart Y. McDougal, *Ezra Pound and the Troubadour Tradition* (Princeton, N.J.: Princeton University Press, 1972), p. 22.
40. Ezra Pound, *The Spirit of Romance*, pp. 26-27.
41. *Literary Essays of Ezra Pound*, p. 74.
42. Joseph T. Shipley (ed.), *Dictionary of World Literature* (Totowa, N.J.: Littlefield, Adams & Co. 1972), p. 372.
43. N. Christoph de Nagy, *The Poetry of Ezra Pound: The Pre-Imagist Stage*, p. 125.
44. T.S. Eliot,"Ezra Pound His Metric and Poetry," *Ezra Pound* ed. J.P. Sullivan (Harmondsworth: Penguin Books, 1979), p. 71.
45. *Ezra Pound, The Spirit of Romance*, p. 22.
46. *The Literary Essays of Ezra Pound*, pp. 110-14.
47. Hugh Kenner, *The Pound Era* (London: Faber and Faber, 1972), pp. 78.82.
48. Stuart Y. McDougal, *Ezra Pound and The Troubadour Tradition*, pp. 90-91.

49. *Literary Essays of Ezra Pound*, p. 171.
50. Hugh Kenner, "Introduction," *The Translations of Ezra Pound* (London: Faber and Faber, 1970), p. 18.
51. *Ibid.*, p. 101
52. Quoted in Kenner, *op. cit.*, p. 100.
53. Joseph T. Shipley ed., *Dictionary of World Literature*, p. 197.
54. Ezra Pound, *Personae* (New York: New Directions, 1971), p. 48.
55. Charles Norman, *Ezra Pound* (London: Macdonald, 1969), p. 76.
56. Ezra Pound, *The Spirit of Romance*, p. 14.
57. Christine Brooke-Rose, *A ZBC of Ezra Pound*, p. 89.

4

Poems 1913-20: The Art of Equations and Literary Accomplishments

After *Umbra* (1920) which contained poems written from 1908 to 1912, and in spite of his great poem *Mauberley* (1920), Pound's reputation as a poet remained almost eclipsed. Because, after 1912, Pound became actively occupied with the study of technical accomplishments of writing poetry. He wanted to bring a change in the situation of his time and create some modern movements in poetry. The period suffered from poetic vacuum and no one was acknowledged a serious poet of Pound's generation. Even Pound failed to publish his major works for eight years. He did not have any response from publishers in America and England.

But in continuation of his involvement with Imagism, Vorticism, Chinese ideogram, and Translations, Pound, from 1913 to 1926, wrote a number of poems which manifest adequacy and development in his style and mode of expression. During this decade he wrote *Lustra* (1916), *Cathay* (1915), *Homage to Sextus Propertius* (1917) etc. and finally brought out the publication of his complete poems in *Personae: The Collected Poems of Ezra Pound* in 1926 published by Liveright of New York.

With the publication of *Personae* (1926), Pound appeared to be a new poet and he evoked good response from writers and poets. The collection was immediately reviewed by a number of writers who tried to assess the work in critical perspective. Ford Madox Ford, W.C. Williams, and Richard Aldington reviewed the collection and accorded praise.[1]

Personae (1926) is a major collection of Pound's poems which were written from 1913 to 1920 and which he wanted to keep in circulation for their relevance to the times. It contains some poems which were already published in early collections. *Hugh Selwyn Mauberley* is also included in this collection; it is one of the most important mature poems of Pound. The main concern of the present chapter is to study the important poems not included in *Umbra* (1920), poems from *Cathay* (1915), *Lustra* (1916), *Homage to Sextus Propertius* (1917), poems which Pound wanted to keep in circulation and included in *Personae* (1926).

The poems undertaken for study in this chapter were composed when Pound was preoccupied with theories of vorticism and ideogram. Most of these poems are creative translations from Chinese classics, Provencal poetry and Latin literature. These translations have a continuity of Pound's use of persona and variety of masks, through which the dead past comes alive and the protagonist presents a criticism of the contemporary society of the model author. There are very short poems, too, which have the quality of pictures in art galleries; such poems are mostly epigrams developed from Japanese and Greek translation. These poems are predominantly visual in imagination though his pre-occupation with melos and discontinuous melos (melopoeia is Pound's word), continues.

In these poems Pound exhibits his maturing talent. Remy de Gourmont, Ford Madox Ford, and Fenollosa had already sharpened his poetic mind and enabled him to use the language as an adequate equation of emotions, with precise and ideographic presentation. His study of Horace, Martial, and Catullus provided him with the use of ironical tone and the satirical mode of expression. If the Chinese poetry helped Pound to get the ideogrammic style, the study of propertius in Latin taught him the art of criticism in poetry.

The poems of *Lustra*, *Cathay*, and *Blast* are mostly translations. But *Lustra* poems present a mode of experience that carries great literary traditions of past writing. Most of the poems in *Lustra* are lyrical, imagistic, and satiric in their ironic mode of expression. They remind the reader of the style of Catullus, Martial and Theophile Gautier. Several of the poems reflect contemporary mentality, social modes, and manners. They are marked by *moeurs contemporaines* and produce the combined effect of hardness and coolness. These poems, which are ironical, ideographic, precise, colloquial, and complex in presentation, paved the way for the composition of an endless poem, the *Cantos*. In addition to composing the poems of *Lustra*, Pound was simultaneously writing some of his Cantos right from 1917. The poems of *Lustra*, thus, can be seen as preparing Pound for a mental attitude which can easily bear the complexity of the form and textural density of the *Cantos*.

Cathay (1915) also contains some very important poems. Most of the poems of this section belong to the art of Chinese perceptivity that Pound learnt from Chinese poetry via Ernest Fenollosa.

The Chinese idogram, which exposes the image with its moving and dynamic properties, generally deals with juxtaposition of facts. The *Cathay* poems are marked by imagistic style and involve the art of superpository technique in the use of images. From imagism and Chinese classics Pound has learnt a kind of discipline which enables him to have control over the use of words.

We have already discussed Pound's imagism and his other critical theories in the opening chapter. Therefore, in order to avoid repetition we need only the briefest possible mention of its main characteristics. Imagism was a discipline which enabled Pound to have a precise, prose-like, and objective art of presentation of ideas and emotion in a poem. It also helped him forge a new foundation for the twentieth century poetry with interpretative, austere, and direct method of expression.[2] Pound was primarily concerned with presentational theory of art. His main aim was to get precision and condensation in the language with musical properties of speech rhythm. In early summer of 1912, he came out with three principles which aimed at achieving objectivity.[3] His imagist theory, in short, stressed the need of a real language, and the image was treated as a medium of presentation of ideas and emotion in visual and precise manner.

In the course of a couple of years Pound dissociated himself from the school of Imagism, as it failed to produce the kinetic effect and stuck to the mere use of fixed values. He discovered the theory of energy and mobility in Wyndham Lewis's Vorticism, which rendered shape, relationship, boundary of ideas and kinetic force in the poem. The Chinese poetry perfected it with the verbal idea of action, condensation, and visual presentation.

The Japanese poetry further enabled Pound to cultivate the use of image in a poem. It provided him with the art of using the superpository technique in which one image is placed on top of the other. This stylistic device combined the qualities of ideograph and condensed exploration of meaning. The images used in the context of Japanese imagism had a wide scope and developed as the technique of juxtaposition in which the use of a chain of images present a modicum of similar and dissimilar pictures and ideas. Metaphors appear in contrast. We shall, therefore, study some short poems which manifest these qualities, poems such as *In a Station of the Metro, Shop Girl, The Encounter, The Garden, Women Before a Shop, L'Art, 1910, Tame Cat, The Bath Tub* and some others which originally belonged to *Lustra* (1916). They were written from 1913 to 1915. These poems correspond somewhat to the Chinese poems of *Cathay* (1915).

In a Station of the Metro is a short poem of two lines:

> The apparition of these faces in the crowd;
> Petals on a wet, black bough.[4]

The poem is like a haiku of Japanese poetry. A haiku consists of three lines in which seventeen syllables are present. In the first line there are five syllables, in the second line seven syllables, and in the third line, five syllables. The form presents the method of precise expression. The poem was originally written in thirty lines. Six months later, it was reduced to half its size, and after a year it was presented in two lines. Pound tried to present in it the condensed exposure of his experience.

He has given an account of his original metro experience, which gave rise to the poem:

> Three years ago in Paris I got out of a 'metro' train at La Concorde, and saw suddenly a beautiful face, and then another and another, and then a beautiful child's face, and then another beautiful woman, and I tried all that day to find words for what that seemed to me worthy, or as lovely as that sudden emotion.[5]

Pound found an equation to present his experience through colours latent in words. He realized the importance of the use of language to present the visual and the role of the poet as the painter.

The second line "Petals on a wet, black bough" presents an image which is capable of suggesting a number of things. This line (indeed, the whole poem) has no verb. There is no sentence, objects which render precise ideas and emotion are put together. The "petals" and "bough" are natural objects.[6] The "petals" are identified with the "apparition of these faces." The two types of objects, different in kind, are fused into one identity by being juxtaposed. Both the "apparition" and the "petals" are visual; one human, the other vegetable. Even though "faces" are associated with "petals," the apparition, at the same time, suggests some kind of ghostly experience, and this in spite of the biographical evidence that Pound associates the faces with beauty. One may call the faces apparitional because associated with the crowd. The poem presents fleeting glimpses of faces, and hence apparitional, appearing and then soon disappearing. The faces appear and then get hidden in the crowd. The "crowd" and the "wet, black bough" are, likewise fused, into one identity.

The first line states the subject of the poem, the "apparition of these faces"; the "petals" are an image superposed on it. The "apparition" is not specific in its presentation of faces; or the faces themselves are not specific in presentation. Nor are the petals specific. The wet and bough, however, is something concrete. The criticism of the poem by Wai-lim Yip is of considerable significance:

> It does not say whether the faces are beautiful, fearful, sunken, tragical, but it suggests them all. And the gist of the moment so captured is juxtaposed with a natural scene. The strong identification of the faces with the petals on a wet, black bough is enforced by the selected epithets of "emotional apparitions" of bleak, a quality that corresponds with, and emerges into the word apparition.[7]

A haiku, as said earlier, is made of seventeen syllables. *In a Station of the Metro,* though it appears to be a haiku, consists of nineteen syllables. The limitation of seventeen syllables is done away with. The rhythm is the rhythm of speech, with two phrases of irregular length as its units. It may correspond to the emotion of the narrator. What kind of emotion? Impingement that fleeting beauty, human and/or natural, makes on the mind. The cadence in the words "crowd" and "bough" constitutes the rhyme of identical vowels. The semantic rhythm consists of five units in the whole of the poem: "The apparition/ of these faces/ in the crowd/ petals/ on a wet, black bough." Under the influence of Pound, many modern poets have composed poems in terms of semantic and phonological phrases, or what Pound calls musical phrases. W.C. Williams and E.E. Cummings, to name just two, have used such "typographical device."[8]

An early version of the poem is called *Piccadilly,* which was not included in *Personae* because of the poem's weaknesses. Nonetheless, the poem, shows the progress of Pound's exercise. *Piccadilly* reads as follows:

> Beautiful, tragical faces,
>
> Ye that mere whole, and are so sunken,[9]

This version is completely changed in *In a Station of the Metro.*

The poem *Fan-Piece, for Her Imperial Lord* has the short form of haiku:

> O Fan of White silk,
>
> Clear as frost on the grass-blade,
>
> You also are laid aside.
>
> (*Personae,* p. 108)

The poem was written before Pound's involvement with Fenollosa's study of the Chinese characters. In this poem, Pound condenses and presents only three lines of Giles's version. The situation is that the Emperor forsook his mistress, and she sent him a silk screen on which her sad feelings were inscribed.[10] In the original poem she suffers from sadness as she felt neglected by her lover, the Emperor. H.A. Giles compares their love with snow and frost. The white colour of the fan also suggests the short life like that of a dew.

Pound compresses the expression of emotion in mere three images, which are used in the three lines of the poem. The first line of the poem presents two things: fan and silk. The second line, again, consists of two images: frost and grass blade. The grass blade provides a situation which clarifies the position of the first image. It suggests short existence of frost. The transistoriness of frost is linked up with fan which is only useful for a season. The third line is full of subtle and intricate explorations of relations and identity. "You are also laid aside" becomes emphatic in tone with the intensifier "also". Pound has correlated the ironic and tragic dimensions of anguish and suffering. The fan is no more useful as the beauty of the lady shows its transistoriness. The fate of the woman and the fan are presented in one image. The comparison brings the real subtle meaning with melting frost, and the use of fan as a toypiece is the image for the unstable beauty of the woman.[11] The tone of the woman is that of a sufferer.

Pound's other poems with the Japanese technique present images which belong to nature. *After Ch'u Yuan, Liu Ch'e, Ts'ai Chi'h* are associated with nature. The poem *After Ch'u Yuan* is a good poem which Pound wrote as an exercise in the Chinese model.

Ch'u Yuan was a minister under Huai-wang. The tone of the Chinese version is sadness[12] but in Pound's version it is concerned with delight and happiness. He depicts a situation which deals with a two-fold vision of beauty. One is represented by Chinese gods with the attributes of pagan deities. The other is concerned with the appearance of maidens. Two images, "silver blue flood" and "ivory cars" describe the visual movement of the procession. The presentation of the maidens and grapes with leopards combine the Chinese and pagan gods together. The "glade" and "thicket" repeat the "wood" image of the first line. The forest appears with the beauty of nature. The narrator addresses his friend who shares his sense of surprise. The colloquial tone makes the voice very informal. The beauty of the maidens and the gods is personal.

The last line shows the dramatic ecstasy which emphasizes the speaker's association with the maidens' procession. The presentation is rendered in modern diction; it also points out the effect of the "ivory cars" and "silver blue flood." The poem presents colours and a procession.

Ts'ai Chi'h is a short poem that consists of only three lines:

The petals fall in the fountain,
    the orange-coloured rose-leaves,
Their ochre clings to the stone.

(*Personae*, p. 108)

These three lines deal with three images. The depiction of natural beauty through petals and fountain are supplemented with the idea of action in "fall." The third line of the poem presents the setting of the earth with colours which enhances the vision of beauty of the earlier two lines. The word "ochre" stands for the accumulated effect of colours as found in a particular kind of the earth. The images of the petals and the fountain are placed on the image of ochre "clinging to the stone." The petals and rose-leaves stick to the stone in the water.

The poems written in the haiku style belong to different literary traditions. The two poems, *Alba* and *April* have Ovidian beauty and Provencal exactness. *April* is a short poem which consists of five lines. The poem begins with an epigraph: "Nympharum membra disjecta," and then come the five lines:

Three spirits came to me
And drew me apart

To where the olive boughs
Lay stripped upon the ground
Pale carnage beneath bright mist.

(*Personae*, p. 92.)

The first four lines in the poem deal with mere facts. But the last line makes us feel the profundity of feelings that the protagonist presents with objects. The Latin epigraph "Nympharum membra disjecta" belongs to Ovid's *Metamorphoses*, III. It is concerned with Pentheus who was slaughtered and torn to pieces. Autonoe tore off his arms and threw them away. He looked to his mother helplessly. His limbs looked like autumn leaves which are stripped from the tree. The poet presents the suffering of the mythological character and identifies himself with him as a sufferer. The sadness is produced in the last line.

The three ghosts in the first line refer to three souls.[13] The spirits point out, to some extent, to ghostly appearances. The images of olive boughs lying stripped on the ground depict nakedness and barrenness. The action becomes visual as the bright mist is startling. The last line brings a combined effect of sharpness and precise expression. The poem can be compared to the poem *In a Station of the Metro,* in which "crowd," "faces," and "apparition" appear as synonyms for ghostly faces. The naked "olive boughs" beneath other trees, which contain flowers and fruits, present the image of petals clinging to the "wet black bough" of the metro poem. The comparison is evocative, yet it presents a similar analogy of the exploration of facts. The "spirits" in *April* resemble "apparition"; and "bright mist" of flowers suggests "something infinitely delicate and desirable, now lost for ever."[14] The poem *April* can be studied like *The Return,* in which spirits appear as the main characters of the poem and the protagonist expresses his surprise. In *April,* "Pale carnage beneath bright mist" shows its clarity when it is associated with the epigraph "Nympharum membra disjecta," scattered limbs of the nymphs.

The use of colon in the end, in the fourth line, suspends the spontaneity. The pause creates suspense. The "olive bough" lying on the ground looks like torn limbs of the king who defied Bacchus. Pentheus was the son of Echion. He always looked down on gods. He went alone to Cithaeron, a mountain, meant for the sacred rites. When he was crossing the valley on his way to the mountain, in the dense forest, his mother and two other spirits wounded him, cut his limbs into pieces, because they failed to recognize him.[15] The last images, "Pale Carnage" and "bright mist," present the picture of a field, filled with dead bodies. The "pale carnage" points out the pale appearance of spirits. The poem is evocative and an example of condensed meaning.

Alba presents "typical imagist fragments:"[16]

As cool as the pale wet leaves
Of lily-of-the-valley
She lay beside me in the dawn.

(*Personae*, p. 109)

This poem is a final version which emerged out of several texts. There has been an anonymous text of the poem in Provencal:

Quan lo rossinhols escria
ab sa par la nueg el dia,
yeu suy ab ma bell' amia
ios la flor,
tro la gaita de la tor
escria: drutz, al leuar!
qu'ieu vey l'alba el iorn clar.

When the nightingale to his mate
Sings day-long and night late
My love and I keep state
In bower,
In flower,
'Till the watchman on the tower
Cry

"Up : Thou rascal, Rise,
I see the white,
Light[17]

Pound first translated the poem into prose. "When the nightingale cries to his mate, night and day, I am with my fair mistress amidst the flowers, until the watchman from the tower cries 'Lover, arise, for I see the white light of the dawn, and the clear day."[18] The Provencal version of *Alba* presents the natural world with the nightingale, the lady and the watchman. The delightful psychic experience is frustrated by the dramatic excitement as dawn appears. In the Provencal version the last three lines present the climax: "Up! Thou rascal, Rise,/ I see the White/light."

But Pound's rendering "She lay beside me in the dawn," is a condensed presentation of the whole experience of the lover. The rising tone of the protagonist in the first line and in the polysyllabic phrase, "lily-of-the-valley," ends with the confessional tone of the third line.

The soft liquid in the words, cool, pale, leaves, lily, valley and lay, provides a soothing phonetic experience. The predominant liquid in the first two lines causes the soft sound and exposes the delicate sense of calmness. The images present a kind of elegance of natural surrounding.

The short Imagist poems as discussed in preceding pages deal with the use of images as a stylistic device. It is also concerned with the proper employment of words and their mode of communication in precise, condensed and evocative manner. But the translation of Chinese poems broadens the field of the Imagist world. The most important translations of Ezra Pound belong to *Cathay* (1915). They seem to be the by-product of Pound's involvement in the Imagist movement. It was Imagism which inspired Pound to proceed to other experiments and traditions of oriental literature, to find out the exact art of presentation. Pound has, through his translations, enriched English poetry, and has transplanted a kind of foreign sensibility into his own. As a writer of the poems of *Cathay*, Pound is an inventor of Chinese poetry for his English readers, because his translations bring out the excellence of Chinese poetic traditions. His translations are translucencies.[19]

Most of the *Cathay* poems were written in the year when Pound was working on the manuscript of Ernest Fenollosa. The poem bears, thus, an influence of ideas and association of thoughts that Pound came to read in the Chinese manuscript. Hence, these translations exhibit a phase of the development in Pound's poetic career, as he learnt more about the art of presentation and verse. Pound learnt, from Chinese poetry, extreme clarity, simplicity, directness, realism, mysticism, humaneness, and the beauty of natural vision.[20]

In the Chinese language the word stands as a character, which also contains one final consonant and one initial consonant. In the matter of rhyme and metre, there are four types of Chinese verse: *Shih, fu, tz'u* and *ch'u*. The first kind of verse, *shih*, is used in folk songs. It deals with a definite line length. The *tz'u* provides a befitting tune. The *fu* possesses chanting quality and deals with presentation of external objects of nature. The *ch'u* is like *tz'u*.[21]

The first poem of *Cathay* that we intend to study is *Song of the Bowmen of Shu*. It is a war poem, like another war poem, *Lament of the Frontier Guard*. The first poem deals with the Chinese soldiers who fought against their enemies. They were far away from their home. In the battle-field, they felt hungry and thirsty, and they were always doubtful about their return home. In these two war poems "there is a feeling of great involvement with war which inspired Pound to write the two poems."[22]

Song of the Bowmen of Shu is a version of Mao-Shih, II, 9.8a (Fang) which was translated in 1871 by Legge in *The Chinese Classics* (Vol. 4, part 2).[23] The poem appeared in many versions, and Pound finally rendered it into English, taking help from notes of Fenollosa. The poem is remarkable for its natural setting, which presents the desolation and barrenness. The persona of the poem is concerned with war soldiers who are busy in fighting but their mental vision makes them remember the homely joys of their native place. The persona in plural exposes the anguish and melancholy of a community. The protagonist suffers from drudgery and isolation. The poem begins with a natural object, "fern-shoots" which seems to be less alluring to soldiers. They are fighting on a foreign soil. They express their mental and physical suffering:

> Sorrowful minds, sorrow is strong, we are hungry and thirsty.
> Our defence is not yet made sure, no one can let his friend return.
>
> (*Personae*, p. 127)

The poem is divided into three parts. The first deals with the facts of discomfort caused by Mongols and foemen "Ken-in." The second part reflects the physical and mental suffering. The third part presents the effect of nostalgia.

The protagonist of the poem faces evils of the war as they are experienced in all wars. The speaker of the poem presents his experience along with that of his fellow-sufferers in conversational tone: "We are," "we have," "we grub," "we say," "we go," etc. are used in every line which lend stress on the effect of the narrative tone of the poem. The poet gives a modern temper to the whole situation. The extreme simplicity and clarity appear in objects. The images as "fern-stalks," "tired horses," willows "drooping with spring," "snow," etc. present the anguish and disparaging attitude. "Three battles a month" presents the feelings of exhaustion. The narrator presents a universal reality, weariness, and insecure feelings of the soldier, willing for the peace of domestic establishment.

In his presentation of war details Pound uses the poetic object as revelation of facts. He changed the unwanted details of war. Hugh Kenner feels that Fenollosa in his version uses the word "horses tied" which Pound changed as "tired" and the change was for the better, an improvement.[24] Pound presents the deadness with living objects of nature. The description of the tiresomeness of horses posits the emotional correspondence of suffering with human tragedy which makes the readers realize the state of affairs of "sorrowful minds." The feelings of loneliness, monotony and gloominess are aptly rendered by Pound in the following lines:

> When we set out, the willows were drooping w :h spring,
> We come back in the snow,
> We go slowly, we are hungry and thirsty,
> Our mind is full of sorrow, who will know of ou grief?
>
> (*Personae*, p. 127)

Lament of the Frontier Guard presents the same facts of depression through various images which are all drawn from nature. As the title indicates the poem is a "Lament." Hence the tone of the poem is elegiac and a kind of melancholy subdues the tone of the narrator of the poem. The Guardman posted on 'North Gate' narrates his plight with geographical awareness of desolated boundary of the territory.

A set of four poems in *Cathay (Separation on the River Kiang, Taking Leave of a Friend, Leave-Taking Near Shoku* and *The City of Choan*) has a common epigraph for them and an introductory note. These poems present a group of men who were talented and had an aesthetic sense of life. They were civil servants and were sent to far places.

The epigraph of the four poems is an important key to the theme of these poems. The epigraph has been taken from the poem of a Chinese poet Wang Wei, who is also known as Omakitsu in Japanese. He died in A.D. 759 and Pound regards him as an "eight century Jules Laforgue Chinois".[25] The epigraph refers to a traveller who shows his readiness to go to the gates of Yang Pass in Kansu province. The speaker, in the epigraph, advises the traveller to drink wine before his departure because he will encounter hardships and calamities. The verse form of the epigraph shows its lyrical qualities in spontaneous flow of the sentences. It consists of triple alliteration; and every line emphasizes the sound "n" in rain, inn, greener and wine. The liquid in "light" and 'r' in "greener" produce music.[26]

Separation on the River Kiang is the first poem of the set. The title of the poem points out its theme. The first line of the poem refers to Ko-in which in Chinese is *Ku-jen* meaning thereby friends. The reference belongs to Meng Hao-Jan, the eighth century "poet and recluse."[27] The friend goes to west from Ko-kaku-ro. The second line of the poem presents a river with scented mist. The natural beauty is felt through "smell." The poem becomes sensuous. The visual and scented atmosphere presents a combined effect in the word "blurr." The next line brings the immediacy of reverse exposure of the ideogram. The contrast shows Ch'ang Chiang, the long river, with its vast boundary, whereas the poet Ko-iin is sailing alone. He is companionless. The gloom appears in the remark of the speaker: "And now I see only the river." The river, though full of scented mist, looks like a vast land.

Taking Leave of a Friend is concerned with the theme of departure. There are many versions of the poem in Chinese which have been translated by H.A. Giles and Li Po. Li Po and H.A. Giles show the major difference in treatment of the theme. The version of Li Po presents visual images and Giles's version deals with emotional depth of the protagonists. But Pound rebuilds the whole poem in a few images which are startling, penetrative and precise. The version of Li Po is unevocative:

> Green mountain across north wall
> White water surround east city
> This place must make parting
> lone boat-awning ten-thousand li march
> floating cloud journeying man thought
> setting sun old friend memory
> waving hand from here depart
> hsiao hsiao horse neigh.[28]

Pound's poem contains only two stanzas. The first part of the poem is concerned with details and facts of the situation. "Blue mountains," "White river," "thousand miles of dead grass," present the natural world. The poem is in the conversational tone. The persona converses with the other man who seeks separation from the narrator of the poem.

The second stanza is full of startling images:

> Mind like a floating wide cloud,
> Sunset like the parting of old acquaintances
> Who bow over their clasped hands at a distance.
> Our horses neigh to each other
> as we are departing.
>
> (*Personae*, p. 137)

In the first line the poet uses a metaphor which is interpretative; and the image of the sun in the second line presents shades of meanings. The poet presents 'horses' making response to human beings. Human suffering is shown in other objects like sun, mind and horses. Pound makes horses to express emotions in neighing. He presents the visual images as found in Chinese.[29]

Leave-Taking Near Soku deals with the theme of exile. The separation in this poem takes place near Shoku, which refers to "the modern state of Ssuchuan."[30] The first king of Shu, Tsa'an-ts'ung built many roads. Pound mentions it in the epigraph, in the poem. The poem begins with a dramatic presentation. The protagonist is referring to a generalized experience of others. The first two lines give us the description of the roads with mountains on both sides. The narrator mentions "sweet tree" in the province of Shensi, bursting boughs and the beautiful scenery. But the last two lines bring the contrast with simple suggestion of ironic tone:

> Men's fates are already set,
> There is no need of asking diviners.
>
> (*Personae*, p. 138)

The subtle feelings are dramatically presented in these two lines. Chung Ping was a fortune teller. If the suffering is the lot, it is predestined. Diviners need not foretell it.

The last poem of this set is *The City of Choan*. The poem deals with the process of decay and ruins of the city, and the images of the "phoenix," "flowers," "grass," "mountains" present the beauty of the natural world in contrast to the grandeur of passing beauty.

Exile's Letter is a long poem. It refers to a letter of the great poet Li Po (A.D. 701-762). He was once exiled in 760 A.D., and during his exile, he wrote a letter to the war councillor of Sho in which the poet recollects his companionship with him. The poem narrates the long association of the poet with the councillor in the form of a memoir. It is a long poem of "major personae"[31] of Ezra Pound. The presentation of facts is through various stanzas. The end is remarkable for its dramatic exploration of ideas. It tells that the letter has to go to a thousand miles. The poem deals with the sweet remembrance of the past that exposes agony and bitterness. The speaker in the poem is confronted with two aspects of time–past and present. The speaker deals with the theme of time, and the technique is narrative. The poem is written in conversational form. But the persona is not a fictional character. It is a real character. He is a Chinese poet. But his suffering becomes the emotional semblance of narrator's suffering.

The poem can be divided into many phases. The first part deals with the Chancellor Yuan who hails from Loyang. The persona holds his friend in great esteem because the Chancellor built an inn at Ten-Shin.[32] The speaker of the poem remembers his good days spent in the company of his friend, the Chancellor Yuan. He also remembers the happy moments enjoyed with other people who reached them by crossing the sea and mountains.

The second part of the poem begins after the end of happiness as their separation takes place. The tone of the narrator changes. The spokesman reminds his friends about the torture and pain he had to bear when they parted with each other. The image presents the anguish in a moving picture of things:

It is like he flowers falling at Spring's end
    Confused, whirled in a tangle.

What is the use of talking, and there is no end of talking,
There is no end of things in the heart.

(*Personae*, p. 136)

The natural objects, in the end of the poem, present the tone of sadness. The evocation presents maximum meanings. The second part of the poem presents details of onward journey through thousand valleys, and natural objects demonstrate the beauty in images as "silver harness," "reigns of gold," "bright flowers and pine wood." These images express the loveliness of the natural surrounding which correspond to the mood of the speaker. The narrative tone gets abruptly smothered as the mood changes. The nostalgia exposes the hidden meaning:

I had to be off to So, far away over the waters,
You back to your river-bridge.

(*Personae*, p. 135)

The expression "to So" means everything and conveys gestures and motions of anguish and sad feelings.

The third part deals with happy memory of the past. The description of the internal decoration, dynastic temple, boats, water and song, are full of sensuous images. The partition is mentioned in the third line. The protagonist asks the boy to dispatch the letter to his friend.

The poems of *Cathay* are good translations of Chinese poems. But critics find out many examples of errors, deviations, misadventures, and mistranslations.[33] Some of the critics find glaring errors in the use of noun, proper nouns, syntax and structure. The question of Pound's fidelity as a translator is controversial. Pound's translation of the Chinese poems via Fenollosa shows his efforts to demonstrate the art of presentation and the use of language in right perspective. His translations are creations as well as criticism. They deal with new forms of poetry and techniques.

The poems of *Cathay* belong to Chinese traditions which lent a new mode to the use of emotion, ideas and language. Pound achieved a "balance and harmony between the relics of an ancient oriental culture and the sensibility of a modern

Western poet in the time of the first great war of the twentieth century."[34]

Most of the poems of *Lustra* are translations from Greek, Latin, and Provencal poetry. The translated poems are lyrics, satires and criticism, The poems from Provencal and Latin versions are Pound's exercise in the techniques of persona which enables Pound to express his own point of view and criticism of the western social milieu. The satirical elements in several poems of *Blast,* which were later included in the collection of *Lustra,* find their roots in the short poems translated from Greek and Latin epigrams. Nonetheless, when *Lustra* came out, it received severe criticism from contemporary writers. The publisher, Elkin Mathews, refused to publish Pound's poems that appeared in *Lustra* as they looked paradoxical, disorderly and defused to him. Harriet Monroe, the editor of *Poetry,* published Pound's *Contemporania* which contained poems such as *The Garret, The Garden,* etc., received damaging letters from scholars who criticized the collection as unpoetic and indescent.[35] Pound reacted sharply. He wrote to Wyndham Lewis: "I appear to be the only person of interest left in the world of art, London. I have had a fine row over *Lustra;* as both Mathews and the printer decline to go on with it on grounds of indecorum...."[36]

The poem *Dance Figure* from *Lustra* has musical qualities and the theme of beauty. It manifests the influence of Swinburne, Bible and Tagore's ideas. The poem begins with an epigraph which has been taken from the Bible, John 2:1 "And the third day there was a marriage in Cana of Galilee."[37] According to the Biblical story, the mother of Jesus asked every one to believe in the utterance of the Lord Christ. A band of women had pitchers full of water. But the guests wanted wine. The Lord Christ performed a miracle. In the guests' dismay the pitchers containing water turned into wine. The marriage ceremony was celebrated with great enjoyment with bride as a matchless dancer. The poet portrays an imaginative character of superb beauty. The fictional and the Biblical, mythical reality merge into each other.

The protagonist presents the lady with the details of her physical beauty. She appears with dark eye, swift feets, rounded arms, bright face, white, almond like shoulders, and brown robe. The poem had a sub-title as "A Thoroughly Sensuous Image,"[38] and the title was cancelled finally before its publication. The narrator of the poem behaves as a lover who praises his mistress as a creation of superb beauty. The lady appears with her physical grace:

> DARK eyed,
> O woman of my dreams,
> Ivory sandaled,
> There is none like thee among the dancers,
> None with swift feet.
>
> (*Personae*, p. 91)

The poem presents different aspects of the beauty of the lady. After her appearance as portrayed by the poet, she appears with all sensuous images of a bedroom that contains a "Gilt turquoise" and "a brown robe" made of gold. She appears as Daphne. The reference of "Tree-at-the-river" points out the metamorphosis of Daphne into a tree. The Daphne-Apollo analogy is reinforced in the next line: "As a rillet among the sedge are thy hands upon me."

The poem suggests a quest for ideal beauty. The poem presents the scene of a bedroom. The narrator appears as a bridegroom who addresses his bride "O Woman of my dreams." The epigraph suggests that the mode of the poem is an epithalamium. The association of images present the beauty and the purity of the lady. The first part of the poem compares the lady with other facts. "There is none like thee among the dancers," "I have not found thee in the tents," "I have not found thee at the well-head," "Thy face as a river with lights," are expressions of the protagonist who tries to establish her as the best amongst others. The second part of the poem provides a positive affirmation of the beauty of the lady. The description of beauty with physical details is also presented in Swinburne's poem *At Eleusis:*

Also at night, unwinding cloth from cloth
As who unhusks an almond to the white
And pastures curiously the purer taste,
I bared the gracious limbs and the soft feet...[39]

The musical structure of the poem belongs to free verse. But in this poem the pattern is different. In Pound's poem the accents are heavily marked as by drum-beats. Pound stressed the use of free verse to make the rhythm beautiful. It should be interpretative, and like the "part of the emotion of the thing."[40]

In the poem, the number of syllables in each line varies from two to nineteen. The number of syllables per strophe varies from fourteen to forty three. Though in this poem, we find the recurring, heavily stressed syllables, there is seemingly little pattern in their arrangement in lines. In the second strophe the line with four stressed syllables is introduced. Though sixteen lines out of twenty-four are three-stress lines, the difference does not affect the pattern.

Surgit Fama is an important poem that presents beauty. The vision of beauty in this poem is pagan which contrasts with modern Christian values. The narrator presents, in the beginning of the poem, the vision of Kore. The poem contains images from the natural worlds as gods, blue and grey sea which present a mysterious world of beauty.

The Garden begins with an epigraph *En robe de parade* which has been taken from Albert Samain's *Au Jardin de l 'Infante* (1893). Samain attracted Pound for his softness. The woman presented in the poem resembles the description of "Infanta of Samain" and has "verbal parallels."[41] But Pound's main concern in this poem is to deal with aestheticism and its social value.

The poem is an ironical presentation of a lady in various contexts. In the first part, she appears with her physical traits; in the second part, the narrator deals with the surrounding of an unhealthy atmosphere; and in the last part, the lady presents an ugly phase of her personality, a most pitiable figure. The picture of the lady is the portrayal of the contemporary London. Ironically the speaker of the poem attacks the social milieu in which Pound lived for years and suffered. London was full of insignificant poets who appeared with their "knots, in their hands, at street corners."[42] The poem tries to present the real London through the woman of the poem.

The Condolence, Tenzone, Salutation the Second and *The Garret* are satirical in tone with highly wrought diction. *The Garret,* which attacks the bohemian attitude and amorous episodes, was set to music by J.C. Halbrooke in 1922.[43] The narrator of the poem presents a sharp contrast between two classes: those who have "friends" but not "butlers" and those who have "butlers" but not "friends." The second strophe presents two images:

> Dawn enters with little feet,
>   like a gilded Pavlova,
> And I am near my desire.
> Nor has life in it aught better
> Than this hour of clear coolness,
>   the hour of waking together.
>
> (*Personae,* p. 83)

The image of dawn has been taken from Sapho, who refers it as "golden-slippered Dawn."[44] This image has been fused with a woman who appears in most of the short poems of *Lustra,* sometimes in amorous forms, but sometimes just as a beauty.

From *Lustra* to *Mauberley* Pound deals with the aesthetic glimpses of cultural beauty. The image of the dawn as a beautiful girl with "little feet" gets associated with gilded "Pavlova," a Russian dancer. The fusion of the two images deal with a subtle presentation of existence of life. The dawn with coolness is meaningful.

Salutation The Second is a poem of self-analysis and turns to the literary world of London. The tradition of the nineties continued in America till 1915; and contrary to the literary taste of the cotemporary period, Pound appeared on the scene with new values of literature with strong resentment against cheap taste and tawdriness. The first part of the poem consists of statement on the contemporary literary world. The second part presents the aesthetics of poets who used quaint devices in poetry. The third part of the poem has a confident tone which echoes the voice of the speaker in *Envoi* of *Mauberley*. The speaker finds a tradition of Waller's song. The protagonist of the poem brings down an onslaught upon the prudery and cheap productions of the *Spectator*, a magazine, edited by John St. Loe Strachey (1860-1927),[45] who also meets with severe criticism in *Blast*. The speaker advocates for the tradition of Cybele and Phallus, who present the myth of fertility and pagan beauty.

The trivial and the serious are brought in contrast which intensify the ironic mood with bitterness. The soft tone changes the mode of expression. The association of real figures like Cordax (reference to Phallus), the fertility goddess Cybele and Loe Strachey are presented in comparison and contrast as they present good values and bad traditions.

The poem *Near Petigord* deals with the character of Bertran de Born and presents three aspects of his personality, he appears as a poet, lover, and warrior. The poem has been written with imagistic and vorticistic characteristics. Though it is written in free verse, it also manifests the influence of Browning.

The first section narrates the tale of indifference of Lady Maent of Montagnac towards Bertran de Born, her lover. The narrator, de Born, is a lover and warrior. The contrast between these two aspects is noticeable: "And I love to see the sun rise blood-crimson." He expresses his love with all sincerity:

> There is a throat; ah, there are two white hands;
> There is a trellis full of early roses,
> And all my heart is bound about with love.
>
> (*Personae*, p. 153)

The second part of the poem shows the speaker grown old. He looks forlorn, weary, and helpless. He writes poems and sends them through a jongleur to a countess who brought about a reconciliation between the poet and his lady. The jongleur wanders from place to place. He meets Aelis (Helis de Montfort), the wife of Bernard de Casnac. He also goes to Ventadour, a lady known as Maria de Turnne, the wife of the vicomete de Ventadorn. He sends his love song to several persons, who wonder whether Bertran de Born really loved the lady of Maent de Montagnac. The section ends with the punishment that Dante awarded to Bertran de Born in his *Inferno*. His beard and head are separated.

The third section presents a solution to the problem of the first part of the poem. Pound juxtaposes images. The protagonist is seen suffering from spiritual and physical crisis. The lady appears as a beautiful vision:

> Gone—ah, gone—untouched, unreachable!
> She who could never live save through one person,
> She who could never speak save to one person,
> And all the rest of her a shifting change,
> A broken bundle of mirrors...!
>
> (*Personae*, p. 157)

The use of blank verse communicates the effect of the tragic end of the speaker as he suffers from internal anguish, mental dejection and psychological repressions. The poem evolves a narrative technique which deals with the details of history, fiction, and vision. He attacks the evils of the medieval period, its feudalism, political intrigues, economic exploitation, and faithless love.[46]

Homage to Sextus Propertius first published in *Quia Pauper Amavi* (1919), is the most important long poem of *Personae* (1926) and contains twelve sections. Propertius was a Roman elegiac poet, who wrote a number of poems concerned with the theme of love for Lady Cynthia. But Propertius attracted Pound for his exposure of evils present in the Roman Empire, equal to the "ineffable imbecility of the British Empire" in 1917.[47]

When Pound brought out his translation of Propertius, he was criticized as a translator. The contemporary critics found Pound's renderings full of errors. Robert Nichols in his article "Poetry and Mr. Pound," published in *Observer*, 11 January, 1920, expressed his opinion that the poem had no synthetic power; and it was full of "harsh levity, spite, cocksureness, innuendo, pendantry, archaism, sensuality."[48] But Wyndham Lewis, John Gould Fletcher and many other critics recognized Pound's work as a modern poem. *Homage to Sextus Propertius,* though a translation from Latin, intends to recreate the history of Propertius and the culture of the Roman civilization analoguous to the present age.

Propertius has written his elegies in four books; but Pound's version begins with the third book. Propertius dealt with his love for Cynthia. Pound's poem creates a character which becomes the persona of both Propertius and Pound at the same time. Pound's main concern in the poem was to bring "a dead man to life, to present a living figure."[49] Pound presents Propertius as a young man of the Augustan period who hated rhetoric and Roman imbecility. As the poem is a recreation of the Latin poem and its elegiac mode, the form enabled him to evolve a narrative technique to deal with other themes. The poem is composed by means of a selection of the best and omission of the repetitions. Pound adapts the framework of ancient or semi-ancient poems to produce a better work as it happens in painting.[50] The poem is a "Homage" by way of an adaptation of the manner of the poet to whom the homage is offered.

Homage to Sextus Propertius is an elegy. Elegy in Greek has a point of "anagnorsis," i.e. discovery of likeness or unlikeness, discovery of the identity and community, and the discovery of the ideal.[51] The four books of propertius deal with Cynthia as a real person and find the elegy as a proper form that deals with themes of jealousy, suffering and death. Propertius shows his dislike of war and yearns for Homeric height. In the last book the lady appears as a vision. Pound's rendering is based on the elegies of the second and the third book.

The poem begins with an epigraph "*Quia pauper amavi*" which refers to Orpheus, from Ovid's *Ars Amatoria* (II, 165), which contains the remark: "*Pauperibus vates ego sum, quia pauper amavi*" ("I am the poet of the poor, because I was poor when I loved.")[52] Besides the theme of love, Pound presents the world of arts, in which an artist should know his commitment.

As the poem begins, the persona confronts the ghosts of two poets Callimachus, a Cyrenaic poet born in 310 B.C. and Philetas, a Greek grammarian whose "love poems influenced Ovid and Propertius."[53] Pound makes an alliance with these two poets and discard Horace and Virgil whose epical poems have dealt with themes of patriotism and political involvement. The narrator of the poem shows his like for the elegiac and ironic mode. The persona goes in quest of his ideal:

SHADES of Callimachus, Coan ghosts of Philetas
It is in your grove I would walk,
I who come first from the clear font
Bringing the Grecian orgies into Italy,
        and the dance into Italy.
Who hath taught you so subtle a measure,
        in what hall have you heard it;
What foot beat out your time-bar,
        What water has mellowed your whistles?

(*Personae*, p. 207)

The speaker expresses his discontent with contemporary poetry which was full of descriptions of war. He discards the "Martian generalities" and "Roman celebrities," because they presented Rome with chauvinistic and patriotic feelings and they were official spokesmen of the empire. The persona wants to remain a poet of the emotion of love. The poet treats the contemporary epic poets of the period of Propertius as "bangers and clangers on the big Roman cymbals, hangers on the martial band wagon, intellectual profiteers like Paul Engle."[54] The section ends with an account of death which destroys everything. Propertius knows his genius and wit that can defy death.

The second section shows its concern with the sanctity of the arts. The poet invokes Phoebus, a lycian god, to speak to Propertius to use his genius for the presentation of love, and not to write poems as Virgilian epics. The protagonist attacks Horace:

> I had rehearsed the Curian brothers, and made remarks on the Horatian javelin
>
> (Near Q.H. Flaccus' book-stall).
>
> (*Personae*, p. 210)

Sectiosns V and VI present traditions of lyrics. The Homage of Pound presents Propertius as a lover, as a devotee of art and thinker. In section V, the speaker talks to his patron Maecenas and tells him the importance of love. The section contains two parts. The first part presents the grandeur of Rome. The poem, in this part becomes a grotesque parody of Virgil. The second part presents the theme of love. The speaker again speaks to Maecenas, a councillor of Emperor Augustus, who patronized Virgil and his fellow poets. Propertius expresses his feeling of love and his concern for it as a great theme of poetry: "*Ingenium nobis ipsa puella facit.*" It is my mistress that makes my wit to write. Pound renders it as: "My genius is no more than girl."[55] The lady inspires the poet, and the feeling of love becomes so powerful that Propertius aspires to achieve Homer's creative vision. Pound makes the speaker not to belong to poets of public oratory. He sums up: "It is noble to die of love, and honourable to remain uncuckolded for a season."

In section VI, the protagonist meditates on his own imagined death. Death kills every one, the victorious and the defeated. The poet brings allusion of two warriors—Marius and Jugurtha. Marius captured Jugurtha and killed him.[56] The epic theme of war and chivalry are satirized. Persephone becomes the symbol of an ideal beauty. The feeling of love and the beauty of woman are considered adequate to make the reputation of the poet lasting:

> Enough, enough and in plenty
>
> Thee will be three books at my obsequies
>
> Which I take, my not unworthy gift, to Persephone.
>
> (*Personae*, p. 219)

Sections III, VI, XI and XII are good elegies translated from Propertius. In these poems Propertius appears as an intellectual poet. These elegies deal with themes of love, death, tragedy and unhappiness. Section III deals with the fidelity of love of the speaker, who also suffers from the fear of death. In the end, the love of the protagonist become pathetic.

Propertius compares his lady with other legendary figures. He prays to Jupiter to save his beloved. If she dies, it will not be possible for him to bear the loss. The beauty of his lady has made other goddesses jealous of her. Even Venus, out of jealousy, has cursed her to suffer:

> Was Venus exacerbated by the existence of a
> comparable equal?
> Is the ornamental goddess full of envy?
> Have you contempted Juno's Pelasgian temples,
> Have you denied Pallas good eyes?
>
> (*Personae*, p. 221)

The poet feels that even Juno, the wife of Jupiter is jealous of Cynthia's beauty. In Section IX, the narrator becomes hopeful that his lady may escape death. This section contains three parts. The first part deals with horrible aspects of nature. The poet presents "scorched laurel" lying in the "fire dust," moon "out of heaven," "black ominous owl," and "veiled lake," as images of frightening death. The speaker expresses his love: "If she dies, I shall go with her." The second part deals with Persephone, who lived with Pluto in the world of the dead. Propertius shows his helplessness. Death is cruel. It kills, everything. Iope, Tyo, and Pasiphae—all died one by one. The third section presents a vision. The poet becomes free from fear.

The tone becomes elegiac in sections XI and XII, respectively. The lady shows her indifference to Propertius who suffers from the betrayal of the lady. The torments of love make him suffer from anguish and torture. The section XI deals with the faithlessness of the lady. As he feels deceived, the poet asks lovers not to involve in love. In the end, the poet, despite the lady's foul display of love, gives solace to his heart and he does not mind the lady's amorous involvement with others:

> All things are forgiven for one night of
> your games.....
> Though you walk in the Via Sacra, with a
> peacock's tail for a fan.
>
> (*Personae*, p. 227)

In section XII, the poet meets his rival Lynceus, a minor poet. He wonders how Lynceus can be a partner of Cynthia's bed, when he has already written about Achelous who fought with Hercules for his beloved Deianira, and at the time of separation Lynceus knew that even horses expressed the sense of grief as they were gifted with the power of human speech.[57] The poet again rejects Virgil, who was able to present only bushes of Thyrsis, pastoral figures in his Eclogues, and cheap love of Corydon.[58] Pound criticizes the Wordsworthian love of nature in Ascraeus' poetry. The poet acclaims:

> My talent acclaimed in their banquets,
> I shall be honoured with yesterday's wreaths,
> And the god strikes to the marrow.
>
> (*Personae*, p. 229)

Sections I, II, V, VI and XII show Propertius's concern for poetry and art; and sections III, VI, XI, XII deal with pangs of love, suffering and fear of death. Propertius also protests against low social morality. As a lover he expresses his feelings. Pound has presented Propertius's elegies in twelve sections in which the protagonist presents his experience as a poet, as a thinker and as a lover. Pound shows the relevance of public poets of Rome with contemporary England in which artists suffered from British imbecile attitude. Pound changes the Latin elegiac diction into conversational form. The poem contains allusions, masks, juxtaposed images, wit, irony and precision. The poem is also a criticism of a creative art. Pound shows his expectations of an artist in a given society. His true Penelope, Flaubert, finds out adequate traditions of poetry in shades of Callimachus and Philetas. The poem ends with examples of love poets, Calvus and Gallus; and the poem, in the beginning, in Section I, presents the poet's awareness, "I ask a wreath which will not crush my head." The elegiac mode makes a discovery of ideal beauty and art.

The study of the poems of *Personae* (1926) present an important phase of Pound's career which shows its preoccupation with many traditions of good literature, experiments and oriental strain. The poems studied in preceding pages also present Pound's poetic adventure which makes him wander into remote regions of Chinese, Latin, Provencal, Greek and Japanese forms. Pound, in his poetic work *Personae* (1926), presents the ideographs of several poets who are the best known examples of great poetic traditions. He translates his poems from Chinese Via Fenollosa, Martial, Catullus, and Propertius. The study of several poems in Chinese, Latin, Greek and Provencal languages, helped Pound to find out proper idioms, and adequate art of presentation of emotions with clear images, precise facts and sophisticated mode of ironic usage. Poems from *Cathay, Lustra* and *Homage to Sextus Propertius* present, in short, the cult of beauty in literature. They present the method of comparison and selection which endeavours to find maximum poetic excellence. Pound has, in these poems, presented a tradition, and a spirit of Renaissance in the modern sense which means "importation of models"[59] of writing. The satirical tone, ideographic images, multiple personae and objective presentation of ideas enabled Pound to write his long poem *Cantos*.

REFERENCES

1. Eric Homberger, "Introduction," *Ezra Pound: The Critical Heritage* (London: Routledge and Kegan Paul, 1972), p. ?
2. *Literary Essays of Ezra Pound*, ed. T.S. Eliot (London: Faber and Faber, 1968), p. 5.
3. *Ibid.* p. 3.
4. Ezra Pound, *Personae* (New York: New Directions, 1971), p. 109. Hereafter references will be made to this source in the body of the text.

5. Ezra Pound, 'Vorticism,' *Fortnightly Review* 96 (1914); quoted in J.P. Sullivan, ed. *Ezra Pound* (Harmondsworth: Penguin Books, 1970), p. 51.
6. Hugh Kenner, *The Pound Era* (London: Faber and Faber, 1972), p. 185.
7. Wai-lim Yip, *Ezra Pound's Cathay* (Princeton: Princeton University Press, 1969), p. 60.
8. K.K. Ruthven, *A Guide to Ezra Pound's Personae (1926)* (Berkeley: University of California Press, 1969), p. 153.
9. Quoted in Wai-lim Yip, *Ezra Pound's Cathay*, pp. 59-60.
10. K.K. Ruthven, *A Guide to Ezra Pound's Personae (1926)*, p. 68.
11. Earl Miner, *The Japanese Tradition in British and American Literature* (Princeton: Princeton University Press, 1958), p. 118.
12. K.K. Ruthven, *A Guide to Ezra Pound's Personae (1926)*, p. 31.
13. *Ibid.*, p. 39.
14. M.L. Rosenthal, *A Primer of Ezra Pound* (New York: MacMillan, 1960), p. 9.
15. *The Metamorphoses of Ovid*, trans. Mary M. Innes (Harmondsworth: Penguin Books Ltd., 1955), pp. 92-93.
16. K.K. Ruthven, *A Guide to Ezra Pound's Personae, 1926*, p. 31.
17. Quoted in Stuart Y. McDougal, *Ezra Pound and the Troubadour Tradition* (Princeton, N.J.: Princeton University Press, 1972), p. 125.
18. Ezra Pound, *The Spirit of Romance* (London: Peter Owen Ltd., 1970), pp. 40-41.
19. T.S. Eliot, "Introduction," *Ezra Pound: Selected Poems* (London: Faber and Faber, 1928), p. 15.
20. Hugh Witmeyer, *The Poetry of Ezra Pound: Forms and Renewal 1908-20* (Berkeley: University of California Press, 1969), pp. 148-50.
21. Richmond Lattimore, "Chinese Poetry," *Dictionary of World Literature*, ed. J.T. Shipley (Totowa, N.J.: Littlefield, Adams & Co., 1960), pp. 52-54.
22. Noel Stock, *The Life of Ezra Pound* (Harmondsworth: Penguin Books, 1974), p. 205.
23. K.K. Ruthven, *A Guide to Ezra Pound's Personae (1926)*, p. 223.
24. Hugh Kenner, *The Pound Era* (London: Faber and Faber, 1972), p. 219.
25. K.K. Ruthven, *A Guide to Ezra Pound's Personae (1926)*, p. 71.
26. Hugh Kenner, *The Pound Era*, p. 201.

27. K.K. Ruthven, *A Guide to Ezra Pound's Personae (1926)* p. 71.
28. Quoted in Ian McLachlan, "The Asian Influence on American Literature as a Basis for Graduate Studies, with particular Reference to the Poetry of Ezra Pound," *Asian Response to American Literature,* ed. C.D. Narasimhaiah (Delhi: Vikas Publication, 1972), p. 43.
29. Hugh Kenner, *The Pound Era,* p. 160.
30. K.K. Rutheven, *A Guide to Ezra Pound's Personae (1926),* p. 72.
31. *Ibid.,* p. 65.
32. *Ibid.,* p. 65.
33. Hugh Kenner, *The Pound Era,* pp. 204-17.
34. Walter Sutton, *American Free Verse: The Modern Revolution in Poetry* (N.Y.: A New Directions Book, 1973), p. 57.
35. Eric Homberger, "Introduction," *Ezra Pound: The Critical Heritage* (London: Routledge and Kegan Paul, 1972), pp. 4-10.
36. *The Selected Letters of Ezra Pound,* ed. D.D. Paige (London: Faber and Faber, 1971), p. 83.
37. K.K. Ruthven, *A Guide to Ezra Pound's Personae (1926),* p. 56.
38. *Ibid.*
39. Quoted in K.K. Ruthven, *A Guide to Ezra Pound's Personae (1926),* p. 26.
40. *Literary Essays of Ezra Pound,* p. 12.
41. K.K. Ruthven, *A Guide to Ezra Pound's Personae (1926),* p. 75-76.
42. Patricia Hutchins, *Ezra Pound's Kensington: An Exploration 1885-1913* (London: Faber and Faber, 1965), p. 50.
43. K.K. Ruthven, *A Guide to Ezra Pound's Personae (1926),* p. 76.
44. *Ibid.,* p. 77.
45. *Ibid.,* p. 210.
46. *Literary Essays of Ezra Pound,* pp. 95-101.
47. *The Selected Letters of Ezra Pound,* p. 231.
48. Quoted in *Ezra Pound: The Critical Heritage,* ed. Eric Homberger, pp. 165-67.
49. *The Selected Letters of Ezra Pound,* ed. D.D. Paige, p. 149.
50. *Literary Essays of Ezra Pound,* p. 10.
51. Abbie Findlay Potts, *The Elegiac Mode* (New York: Cornel University Press, 1967), pp. 50-65.
52. Quoted in K.K. Ruthven, *A Guide to Ezra Pound's Personae (1926),* p. 87.

53. *Ibid.*, p. 90.
54. James Lauglin, "Ezra Pound's Propertius," *Sewanee Review* (Oct-Dec., 1938), p. 86.
55. K.K. Ruthven, *A Guide to Ezra Pound's Personae (1926)*, pp. 105-06.
56. *Ibid.*, p. 108.
57. *Ibid.*, p. 123.
58. *Ibid.* p. 124.
59. *Literary Essays of Ezra Pound*, p. 214.

5

Hugh Selwyn Mauberley: A Poetic Incursion in Twentieth Century Poetry

Hugh Selwyn Mauberley (*Life and Contacts*), a serious poem dealing with the state of contemporary society and arts, was first published by Ovid Press in 1920; later, it was included in *Poems, 1918-1921* and *Personae* (1926). It depicts the crisis of an alarming situation of 1920s. Most of the critics have focused their attention mainly on Pound's eclectic aestheticism and creation of Mauberley as a minor poet. Some have also made a study of Pound's use of persona and the construction of the poem. F.R. Leavis has, however, evaluated the poem as a whole.[1]

The first publication of *Hugh Selwyn Mauberley* in June 1920, met with severe criticism. Edwin Muir considered the poem cryptic, unsatirical, and disappointing.[2] Because of the fact that the poem was divided into two parts, many critics failed to discover any logical progression or scheme. Some regarded the poem as a compiled work of many fragments of sordid feelings. R.P. Blackmur finds it lacking in logic, argument and mythical plot. In his opinion, the work lost its identity in the medium of the poem that considered of phrasing, rhyming, mere echoes and references.[3] But F.R. Leavis, T.S. Eliot and G.S. Fraser look upon the poem as a unified whole and find it a superb creation of a great genius. Eliot remarks:

> It may give surprise that I attach so much importance to *Hugh Selwyn Mauberley*. This seems to me a great poem....I perceive that the versification is more accomplished than that of any other of the poems in this book, and more varied... the poem seems to me, when you have marked the sophistication and

> the great variety of verse, verse of a man who knows his way about, to be a positive document of sensibility. It is a compact of the experience of a certain mask in a certain place at a certain time; and it is also a document of an epoch; it is genuine tragedy and comedy; and it is, in the best sense of Arnold's worn phrase, a 'criticism of life.'[4]

T.S. Eliot's estimation is a judicious pronouncement which has been applied to parts of the poem by others. One thing is clear that the poem belongs to a new mode in English poetry. It is divided into two broad sections which contain a total of eighteen poems. Some of the poems are numbered according to the order in which they occur, and some are placed with their titles and without any numbering. These poems seemingly look unrelated to one another. The first section consists of thirteen poems; it begins with the *Ode* and ends with *Envoi* (1919). The total number of lines in the first section is 245. In the second section, there are only five poems and the total number of lines is 156. The entire poem, thus, consists of eighteen poems of 401 lines.

It is a long poem like *The Waste Land* of T.S. Eliot, and *The Bridge* of Hart Crane. The first part is longer than the second one. The division gives the impression of two separate poems in which the personae of Mauberley and Pound operate simultaneously. The entire poem appears growing without any design and logic. The various poems are without any temporal links. The poem entitled *Mauberley 1920*, which opens the second section, takes off from *Envoi* (1919) of the first section. This may give the impression that the second part of the poem is composed as a result of an afterthought. *Envoi* (1919) is supposed to be a post-script to the poem and presents an idealized picture of a lady. A similar picture of a singing woman is to be found in *Medallian* in the second part. The last poem of the second section, thus, parallels *Envoi* (1919) of the first part. These sections are, therefore, well connected.

Moreover, even if the second section is treated as a fresh note to the first sequence, there will not be any difficulty in finding out a coherent connection. In the two sections, Pound has presented several levels of experience, and the overall title, *Hugh Selwyn Mauberley (Life and Contacts),* suggests Pound's main concern in the poem. It deals with the life of Mauberley, a fictitious character and observer of a moribund socio-cultural milieu. Mauberley is cast in the role of an aesthete in a literary setup of artistic bankruptcy. Mauberley is helpless and ineffective like Eliot's Tiresias or Prufrock. Mauberley speaks in different voices with a view to exposing the modern world. He is self-depreciative even of his own aestheticism. The poem is Pound's farewell to London, bidden twice.

The sequence-pattern of Pound's poem is also to be found in *The Bridge* by Hart Crane, *Song of Myself* by Walt Whitman, and *Paterson* by William Carlos Williams. Eliot's *The Waste Land* shifts from aridity and futility to a spiritual resolution; but Pound does not make religion a solution to the evils; he looks to the artist for a social role. The title of the sixth poem, *Yeux Glauques,* has been derived from a poem by Gautier, *Cerulei Oculi:*

> Sex Yeux, oui le ciel Se reflete,
> Melent a Leur azur amer,
> Que toile una humide pillette,
> Les teintes glauques de la mer.[5]

The word glauques refers to the writers of the nineties. The title of the seventh poem, *Siena Mi Fe'; Disfecemi Maremma* has been taken from Dante's *Purgatorio,* Canto V, where we have the story of La Pia, who was murdered by her husband. Pound's title suggests the pathetic fate of La Pia: "Sienna gave me birth, Maremma Death." There is an analogy between London and Maremma. La Pia is an analogy for the tragic fate of the contemporary artist, such as Lionel Johnson. The tragic note echoes the elegiac mood of the first poem, in which the narrator finds E.P. buried.[6] The titles such as *Brennbaum, Mr Nixon* and, in the second sequence, *Mauberley 1920* and *The Age Demanded* have specific ironic significance. These titles can be regarded as prefaces which project an introductory background to the poems. The poems, which are not given titles, also echo ideas of the same plight, chaos, inhumanity and failure. All the eighteen poems are related to each other thematically.

The first section of thirteen poems can be studied in four patterns.[7] The first three poems constitute the first pattern of images drawn from Homer and Heraclitus to put contemporary morality and desperation in a historical frame. The second pattern deals with the horror of war in poems IV and V. The third pattern delineates the nineteenth century literary history in poems VI and VII. The last pattern is concerned with the contemporary situation and the attitude, a commercialized society in poems VIII-XII. *Envoi (1919)* is a lyric song whose elegiac note refers back to the ironical and sad mood of the section. The five poems of the second part affirm the values already presented in the first section.

In the first section, the title of the first poem, *E.P. Ode Pour L'Election de Son Sepulchre,* is a line from Ronsard's *De L'Election de son Sepulchre.* The line by Pound parodies the source to impart an ironic tinge to the mode of elegiac oration: "Ezra Pound: Ode on the Occasion of Choosing His Burial Place." The title refers to the poet's own imagined burial. In its first publication "E.P." was not there in the title. But in the next edition "E.P." was added to the title.[8] The first poem opens with an epical mode. However, the orational mode of the poem is elegiac and reminds us of Gray's elegy. The Homeric world of Odysseus is used as an image to describe the journey of the poet who was in quest of beauty and sublimity, his Penelope Flaubert. The speaker of the poem feels "out of key with his time."

Pound employs the story of Odysseus and his journey from Troy to Ithaca and the tale of his seduction by Circe as an image for the situation of the contemporary poet. It was a difficult task for Odysseus to complete his journey, as for E.P., who persues his quest persistently for good art and enduring values of literature. This quest theme is continued in both the sections. "Capaneus," who was destroyed by Zeus through a lightning but stood in defiance courageously, is an image for the energy and strength of the poet. The reference to Francois Villon is ironic. He suffered from forgetfulness in his thirtieth year and was banished from Paris, even though he was a distinguished man of letters. Pound's own reputation had suffered neglect for years. The reference to Flaubert suggests perfection in art as the ideal of the poet. His principle of *mot juste* was incorporated in the Imagist theory. Flaubert's was a style concerned with the language that described objects with precision and accuracy. An effort to establish the values of writer like Flaubert is modern classicism. Penelope stands for the goal. The entire poem shows the influence of Bion who wrote pastoral elegies. The effect of ironic tone in the poem is sharpened by the attitude of lamentation.

Pound's experiment in rhythm includes a line from Greek (which I have transliterated in English characters below):

> Idmen gar toi panth, os eni Troie[9]
> Caught in the unstopped ear;
> Giving the rocks small lee-way
> The chopped seas held him, therefore, that year.[10]

The first line (in Greek) has perhaps the same length as the fourth line, and it rhymes with the third. "Troie" rhymes with "lee-way." It seems as though Pound has tried to assimilate a Greek phrase into his verse of musical phrases. But perhaps the Greek rhythm stands apart from the English rhythm of Pound's verse and thereby contributes to discontinuity in rhythm as well as in sense.

The first poem presents the experiences of E.P., who is buried for his quest for beauty and the sublime. The narrator finds the literary setup hostile to traditional values of beauty and sublimity. He finds E.P. was not in harmony with the "half savage country" and the "obstinate isles." The narrator's tone underlines the cultural aridity of London at the time.

The second poem continues the experience of the artist's quest. The third person of the first poem, E.P., however, disappears in the second poem. The narrator, from a distance, speaks in a distant voice, exposes the deteriorating state of arts, religion, and politics in poems II-V. The picture of the age is given neatly and concisely:

> The age demanded an image
> Of its accelerated grimace,
> Something for the modern stage,
> Not, at any rate, an Attic grace;
>
> (*EPSP*, p. 188)

The narrator bemoans the debased taste of the reading public and the bourgeois patrons of art:

> The 'age demanded' chiefly a mould in plaster,
> Made with no loss of time,
> A prose kinema, not, not assuredly, albaster
> Or the 'sculpture' of rhyme.
>
> (*EPSP*, p. 188)

According to A.C. Partridge, the metrical plan of this poem "is relatively simple; it consists of quatrains in a rising rhythm and lines of irregular length. They have plentiful trisyllaic modulation, occasional prosaic lines (2 and 11) and numerous inversions of stress at the beginning of the line (3, 4, 5, 7, 10), often arising from the colloquial emphasis of the speaker (as the repetitions of not in lines 4 and 5). The latter are rhetorical devices known as *epizeuxix* which conversationalists often employ unconsciously."[11]

The third poem portrays the values of modern world by means of its contrast with desirable values. The pagan world of Dionysus and truthful dedicated life of the Christ are contrasted with contemporary superficiality of values:

> The tea-rose tea-gown, etc.
> Supplants the mousseline of Cos,
> The pianola 'replaces'
> Sappho's barbitos.
>
> (*EPSP*, p. 189)

The contrast is continued with reference to Christ and Dionysus, the former representing religious asceticism and the latter pagan fertility cults. Pound found even Christianity lifeless in its later phase. Greek Paganism attracted him for its inherent invisible sublimity:

> Paganism, which at the base of its cosmogonic philosophy set the sexual phenomena whereby Life perpetuates itself mysteriously throughout the universe, not only did not disdain the erotic factor in its religious institutions but celebrated and exalted it, precisely because it encountered in it the marvellous vital principle infused by invisible divinity into manifest nature.[12]

It was Nietzsche who discovered Dionysus in his book *Birth of Tragedy* (1872). For him Apollo symbolized individuality and Dionysus proved a force to blow out the "principium individuationis." Dionysus belongs to the myth of vegetation who had a mortal mother. He died and resurrected; at the celebration in his honour, offerings of blood and flesh were made. The defeat of Dionysus by modern Christianity of "macerations" is lamented by the speaker. For Pound, the metamorphic and fertility rites of Dionysus worked as "metaphors for the process of artistic creation."[13] Christ, too, is placed by Pound on the side of Dionysus; for he stood for certain values. In the absence of desirable values, Pound's world and the barrenness of the present are placed side by side in both the poets. The spiritual and materialistic references juxtapose themselves to pinpoint the scornful tone of the narrator.

Phallic and ambrosial refer to the fertility cults. Caliban stands for ugliness and materialism and replaces the spiritual sublimity suggested by Ariel. Religious values and pagan rites are both annulled by modern materialism. The saintly vision of Christ and the pagan beauty of "Faun's flesh" are both thrown out. "Faun's flesh" used by Pound refers, according to G.S. Fraser, to Elizabeth Siddal, a Pre-Raphaelite beauty as well as to the beauty of the White Goddess.[14] The Greek phrase *to kalon* means "the beautiful," and beauty is now judged by the commercial standards of the market place.

The political evils of the time are under attack in the next stanza. The entire democratic setup has been presented as the fool's paradise, where "All men, in law, are equals," and life is ruled by "an knave or a eunuch." Pound may be attacking, thinks K.K. Ruthven, Woodrow Wilson, who was the President of the United States from 1913 to 1921, and David Lloyd George, who was the Prime Minister of England from 1916 to 1922.[15] Peisistratus was a sixth century tyrant, who was a patron of art and letters. In debased democracy art does not flourish at all.

The last stanza opens with an address to Apollo, who presides over the arts of poetry and music:

> O bright Apollo,
> tin andra, tin eroa, tina theon,[16]
> What god, man, or hero
> Shall I place a tin wreath upon!
>
> (*EPSP*, p. 189)

The address has a tinge of sadness. The sense of loss is mixed with a scornful attitude. These lines are a remarkable presentation of movement of words, use of pun and ironic imitation. Pindar's line—"What man, what hero, What God!" has been ironically opposed to drumbeat rhetoric.[17]

The Greek line from Pindar has been used for a specific ironic setting of words. The word "Tin" is repeated again in the last line which is a pun as well as ironical attack on social and moral degradation. "Tin andra, tin eroa, tina theon"—this line produces a jingling effect, "What man, What hero, What God" of Pindar is reversed by Pound as "What god, man, or hero" who deserves to be honoured with a tin wreath. Pindar becomes a representative of the poets who eschewed the austerity of language and betrayed the social role of artists.[18]

Poems IV and V are an indictment of the war fever and its effects on society. These poems express the horror of the war caused by the follies of false patriotism. Pound shows his dislike for two things: usury and war. The entire picture of war is frightful, full of grief, pain, sorrow and death:

> THESE fought in any case,
> and some believing,
> pro domo, in any case...

Some quick to arm,
some for adventure,
some from fear of weakness,
some from fear of censure,
some for love of slaughter, in imagination,
learning later...
some in fear, learning love of slaughter;
Died some, pro patria,
non "dulce" non "et decor"...
... ...
Daring as never before, wastage as never before.
Young blood and high blood,
Fair cheeks, and fine bodies;

(*EPSP*, p. 190)

The poem has speech rhythm. The colloquial tone and conversational diction contribute to the spontaneity of rhythm. Repetitions are like incantation. The tragedy of the war-dead is touchingly evoked.

THERE died a myriad,
And of the best, among them,
For an old bitch gone in the teeth,
For a botched civilization,

Charm, smiling at the good mouth,
Quick eyes gone under earth's lid...

(*EPSP*, p. 191)

The poet sums up the story of human wastage. The first part of the poem is an attack on the illusions of war, its aspirations, and participation in it. The second part deals with the sense of grief and sadness over death.

People died for the sake of their motherland. Cicero's *"De Domo Sua"* has been mentioned as *"pro domo"*. Some died for their father land. The Horacian line *"dulce et decorum est pro patria mori"* ("it is good and glorious to die for the father land")[19] is an ironic exposure of patriotic zeal. After the war, there was only humiliation, failure, and degradation for the demobilized warrior.

The next four poems have titles. The two poems VI and VII are entitled *Yeux Glauques* and *Siena Mi Fe, Disfecemi Maremma:* they are a commentary on the literary scene of the time. The sixth poem etches out the literary history since the late Victorians, and mounts an attack on the attitude of writers who were spokesmen of philistinism. Gladstone, John Ruskin and Buchanan stand for spurious modern values of art and poetry. They were hostile to Swinburne, Rossetti and Fitzgerald. Pound presents a contrast between the aesthetic ideals of the Pre-Raphaelites and the principle of the Georgians who still looked to Victorian sluggishness. Pound's quest for new ideals shows his zeal. In a letter addressed to Felix E. Schelling he admired a few poets as didactic poets:

> I am perhaps didactic; so in a sense, or in different senses are Homer, Dante, Villon, and Omar, and Fitzgerlad's trans. of Omar is the only good poem of Vict. Era that has got beyond a fame de cenacle. It's all rubbish to pretend that art isn't didactic. A revelation is always didactic. Only the aesthetes since 1880 have pretended the contrary, and they aren't a very sturdy lot.[20]

He also felt convinced that in every art, the revelation is always didactic. So he considered Fitzgerald's translation a good poem of the Victorian period. Gladstone, Ruskin, and Buchanan were advocates of Victorian morality in the sense that they were opposed to the values of the Pre-Raphelites and their view of beauty. Rossetti, Swinburne, and Browning were acceptable to Pound. If Browing provided Pound with the device of communicating emotions through a Persona, Rossetti and Swinburne gave him the art of beautific vision. It is wrong to say that Pound looked to Swinburne for rhythm and sonority. Like Rossetti, Swinburne offered Pound the vision of a beautiful world. Pound admired Swinburne for the virtues of paganism. Pound liked the Dionysian cult in Swinburne and in Rossetti, and in any early essay on "M. Antonius Flaminius and John Keats," admired them for "the intense, surcharged beauty of blood and ivory."[21]

Morris and Rossetti possessed a fascinating and charming Smaragdite medievalism, but Pound preferred the Provencal and Troubadour poets as representing true medievalism. Even though the Smaragdites victorians used victorian English, Rossetti and Swinburne had some living tradition. Pound presents the Pre-Raphaelites to serve a point of contrast with the Philistines and victorianism.

In contrast to the aesthetes first comes Gladstone. He was held in high regard among contemporary writers and poets. Gladstone stood for hypocrisy and pompous values. Ruskin projected a vain morality as enlightenment for the progress of victorian society. "Kings' Treasuries" refers to Ruskin's famous work *Sesame and Lilies.* Gladstone declared Swinburne ineligible for the honour of the poet Laureatship after Tennyson's death. Buchanan was a journalist who, in his *The Fleshy School of Poetry,* criticized Rossetti and other Pre-Raphaelite poets. He was not a serious writer. The Pre-Raphaelite ideal of beauty was embodied in women. Elizabeth Eleanor Siddal was, for the Pre-Raphaelites, one of the embodiments of feminine beauty. The famous painting of Sir Edward Burne-Jones *Cophetua and the Beggar Maid* possessed the beauty of the Pre-Raphaelite sensibility. Omar Khayyam, whose Rubaiyats were translated by Fitzgerald, described beauty as "Thin like brook-water, with a vacant gaze." He was not known to the reading public. The beauty in the Pre-Raphaelite poetry and its ideal preserved in the paintings were condemned by men like Buchanan, who not only stands for Victorian Philistinism but also represents a journalistic approach to literature and poetry. The narrator also attacks the ignorance of contemporary audience which fails to appreciate the ideals of beauty in painting and poetry whose models were drawn from past traditions.

The next few lines deal with the sense of beauty embodied in Mrs. William Morris, known as Jane Burden. The reference is to a poem of Rossetti that deals with a prostitute.[22] Pound's lines run as follows:

> The thin, clear gaze, the same
> Still darts out faun-like from the half-ruin'd face,
> Questing and passive....

'Ah, poor Jenny's case'...

Bewildered that a world
Shows no surprise
At her last maquero's
Adulteries.

(*EPSP*, p. 191-192)

Buchanan had attacked this kind of description in Rossetti in his article *Fleshy School of Poetry* in which he undermined beauty. Buchanan and Ruskin are treated as great moralists who thought of art as moral presentation of things. Gladstone presents hypocrisy, pompousness and shoddiness. To sum up, the aesthetic presentation of beauty in art and poetry was out of key with the spirit of the time.

The seventh poem ironically presents the same situation as rendered in poem VI. In this poem there is a repulsive attack on the writers of Nineties. It is a short poem of five stanzas. The narrator of the poem critically surveys the literary situation. Monsieur Verog, Lionel Johnson and others are presented through the narrator's description. The poem is a combination of sadness and light humour. The title refers to La Pia in Dante. Murdered by her own husband, La Pia spoke to the poet Dante:

Remember me, that am called Piety,
Siena made me and Maremma Undid me,
As well he knows who plighted troth to me
And he set his ring upon my hand toward me.[23]

Monsieur Verog is the fictive name of Gustave Plarr, the author of *Ernest Dowson* and *The Dorian Mood.* His poem *Strasbourg* was published in 1918. Pound met him in 1909. Plarr reappears in Canto LXXIV, in which he talks on mathematics. The significance of the Plarr reference is that as La Pia met Dante in Purgatorio,[24] Plarr met Pound in a literary Purgatory and told him how the poets of the Nineties were done away with by the establishment. Verog indulges in "reveries" and reminisces the past as La Pia. Through the reveries of Plarr several writers of the Nineties are referred to: Rhymers' Club and W.B. Yeats, T.W. Rolleston, John Davidson, Ernest Dowson, Selwyn Image,

Richard Le Gallienne, and Arthur Symons and some others. Some of them were good poets and learned to disown verbosity and the Victorian tone. Lionel Johnson and Newmen were Roman Catholics, but they drank heavily. H(ıdlam was also addicted to drinking; he was a lover of dance. Selwyn Image was a lover of poetry. The lovers of poetry, danc , and religion were not given their due.

The narrator pungently expresses: "Dowson found harlots cheaper than hotels." Literary allusions to figures via Victor Plarr present a Kaleidoscopic scene of the situation in the 1890s. Dante's journey among the dead is implied as a frame and an image to assess the literary scene in many of the poems. This is suggested by Elpenor-Circe, Odysseus-Penelope, Dante-La Pia, Dante-Virgil, Pound-Flaubert, and, in this poem, Mauberley-Nineties images. The shift from La Pia episode to the literary Purgatory of Victor Plarr produces an ironic revelation of facts:

> Dowson found harlots cheaper than hotels;
> Headlam for uplift; Image impartially imbued
> With raptures for Bacchus, Terpsichore and the Church.
> So spoke the author of "The Dorian Mood,'....
>
> (*EPSP*, p. 193)

The narrator feels like an outcast; he is neglected by the young. In his reveries he feels not only sad but "out of step with the decade." The remark of F.R. Leavis on this poem is apt:

> The irony of this might be called flippant: if so, it is a flippancy that subserves a tragic effect. Nothing could illustrate more forcibly Mr. Pound's sureness of touch, his subtle mastery of tone and accent. The poem is one of the most daring things in the sequence–though 'daring' might suggest a possible qualm about it; it is justified by complete success.[25]

Despite Leavis's praise of the poem for its ironic effect and Pound's efficient handling of facts with detached comments, tone, accent, and satire, the poem has not found favour with many critics. Mr. A.L. French is critical of Pound's use of "cool" and "chilling" irony. He finds, in Pound, an inadequate sensibility. He compares Pound's poem to Voltaire's *Candida*, in which suffering is unreal; he finds a reduction of human condition to triviality.[26]

The hollowness that Victor Plarr finds in contemporary literary situation is a common experience of triviality. But French misses the point; in this poem Pound presents the Nineties. The poets of the Nineties are mentioned for certain characteristics of their writings, and some of them were held by Pound in high esteem. He considered Dowson a fine craftsman. Some of the poets of Rhymer's Club were against artificial usage and jingoism.[27] But the poets of the Nineties, too, are under attack in this poem. The past in this poem does not belong to the Homeric world. The ironic effect is produced by La Pia-Dante and Plarr-Pound analogy. The tragic effect is latent in the evocation of spuriousness of religions, and artistic and cultural debunking of society.

The next four poems of the first section present acrid pictures of male literary careerists. Two of the poems deal with female portraits. In poems VIII, IX, and X three stylists bemoan the pathetic world of journalistic writings. The creativity suffered from contemptuous perversion of literary profession. In poems VIII to XII, the speaker critically surveys the contemporary situation of the materialistic shoddiness. Self-imposed exile frustrates the artist-hero who has launched on a literary enterprise. Poem VIII presents the portrait of a Jew, Mr. Brennbaum, who had to live in a society opposed to Jews. He felt discriminated and isolated; he settled in Italy in 1910.[28] He was a stylist in fashion and a dandy. This short poem contains only two stanzas. The portrait given, becomes a living character whose physical details suggest a meticulous fashion stylist. The references of Horeb, Sinai, and forty years allude to meaningful religious facts which Brennbaum found only reserved as "heavy memories." The references are to *Exodus* and *Joshua*. At Horeb Moses saw the burning bush, and Sinai is a mountain where Moses received the Ten Commandments. Israel was the city of the Jews. Its children wandered in exile for forty years. These historical and religious facts expressed themselves through Brennbaum as his private feelings.

Mr. Nixon, based on Arnold Bennett, is the second portrait in acrid style in the next poem. He is a public man. Mr. Nixon is a "typical philistine-artist of the Edwardian age."[29] The opening line of this poem presents the portrait of a fashionable wealthy man. The gilded cabin of his "steam yacht," is the picture of the place where this showy man lived. He is a "successful" writer. For him, as he says, a reviewer is a very important man. He advises the protagonist to write for columns in newspapers and popular magazines. The reference to Dr. Dundas, for Robertson Nicoll, is again satirical. Nixon could not surpass him in cheapness. Fraser describes him sarcastically: "He had a desire to accumulate money as much as Canon Doyle."[30] Nixon is satisfied with tips he gests and does not feel any need to look to the circulation of his works. Nixon as a character, stands for an objectified reality. Pound makes a representative figure of the contemporary literary establishment.

Poem gives us a portrait of Ford Madox Ford, who was a writer with a great stylist, a genuine writer whom Pound met in 1908. When discharged from Army, Ford settled in Sussex. He lived in a dilapidated house. Made of bricks and tiles, the house had a big hole in the roof.[31] Ford settled there to raise pigs. He makes a mention of his meeting with Pound: "For Mr Pound hated the country though I will put it on record that he can carve a suckling pig as few others can."[32]

Ford's talent as a writer was duly recognized after 1950. Unfortunately he lived at a time which was quite unfertile to experimental prose writings. In a letter in 1913, Pound wrote that Ford remained unrecognized. He had repudiated the nonserious Bennetts and Galsworthys of the time.[33] The five portraits we have discussed present luminous details of the age.

The next poem is a short but crisp expression of the cultural devastation. Its theme extends to Poem XII, in which Lady Valentine represents the art of London; and Daphne impinges on the narrator's consciousness of the waste of beauty and art. Poem XI presents a lady with erotic instincts. The woman stands as an embodiment of past values. The first line, "*Conservatrix of*

Milesien," has been taken from a short story written by Gourmount. The phrase "conservatrices des traditions milesinnes" is paraphrased by Pound as "woman the conservator, the inheritor of past gestures."[34] The narrator finds erotic instincts of the lady suppressed. In this poem she symbolizes traditional values. The poet presents a cultural dimension of the female sex.

Gourmount thinks that a lady's "function is to conserve the useful traditions of the species or civilization—in her role, as child-rear and educator, it is she who transmits the cultural heritage, above all its language."[35] In this poem the protagonist attacks Christian moralists who correlate sexual and erotic instincts with theological abatement. "No, 'Milesian' is an exaggeration./ No instinct has survived in her"—these are topical remarks.

Poem XII is a piquant analogy of waste and barrenness. The narrator is conscious of multifarious crises. His consciousness is like that of Prufrock. The picture is Kaleidoscopic and moves from mythology to modern interpretation. The cultural, commercial and artistic values operate in this poem and they infer the sense of waste and futility. The poet presents ideograms:

> "DAPHNE with her thighs in bark
> Stretches towa. J me her leafy hands,"—
> Subjectively. In the stuffed-satin drawing-room
> I await the Lady Valentine's commands,
>
> Knowing my coat has never been
> Of precisely the fashion
> To stimulate, in her,
> A durable passion;...
>
> (*EPSP*, p. 196)

The fist two lines are drawn from Theophile Gautier's poem *Le Chateau du Souvenir.*[36] Pound adopts the first two lines from Gautier and uses them in his own manner. Daphne-Apollo episode also occurs in Ovid, who deals with the transformation of Daphne, into a tree.

The episode of Daphne and Apollo presents a savage act of sexual ravishment. The metamorphic images are placed in an ironic context of inhuman experience. The age denies the value of aesthetic experience and refuses to accord literary recognition to Apollo as a god of poetry and Daphne as a true patroness of the arts. They are only recognized as sexual embodiments. The poet finds Daphne stretching "her leafy hands" subjectively. "Subjectively" suggests that the aesthetic experience in regard to Daphne is confined to the poet alone. Others do not share it with him. She is, for the age a diminished figure.

The narrator gives us the portrait of another woman, Lady Valentine. She appears in an aristocratic style. The portrait of Lady Valentine is drawn after Lady Ottoline Morrel and Lady Geraldine Otter.[37] Daphne is presented to serve a point of contrast with a modern woman who extends her patronage in the most insignificant manner. The device is intended to expose and measure the world of false pretentions of art. Lady Valentine patronizes art and poetry. The ironic situation shifts to gross realism:

> Poetry, her border of ideas,
> The edge, uncertain, but a means of blending
> With other strata
> Where the lower and higher have ending;
>
> (*EPSP*, p. 196)

What a grotesque picture? The patron also claims to conduct the highest cultures. The last four lines of the poem render a sharp realization of the ambivalent attitude towards vulgarity and hostility. Sappho was no more honoured, and the Olympian Muse was derecognized. The "Pierian-roses" were superceded by "half-hose." The Pierian rose refers back to the theme of "The tea-rose tea-gown." The reference of 'Sale of half-hose' against 'Pierian roses' is ironic. In such lines as "her border of ideas/ The edge, uncertain, but a means of blending/ with other strata/ where the lower and higher have ending" details and objects have "ominous precision."[38] The narrator presents a mock-heroic juxtaposition of two female figures. Lady Jane is conscious of her aristocratic position, and Lady Valentine has artistic and cultural passion. Daphne is considered out of place. Journalism has little sense of beauty.

The seven stanzas present a glowing picture. The conflict is between the serious and the trivial, old and new, beauty and cheapness. The narrator juxtaposes the green conception of beauty with the modern notion of bourgeois living. In poems VI to XII, the acrid portraits are like ideograms. They based on real men and women. Each is representative of a very large number of people of the same type.

Envoi (1919) is the last poem in the first section of *Hugh Selwyn Mauberley*. The critics who find discontinuity and unsystematic scheme in the poem doubt the poetic necessity of *Envoi*. They also find the five poems of the second section unnecessary additions. *Envoi* is a poem in lyric tradition. It is written in the manner of Edmund Waller, a seventeenth-century poet. It is a pastiche of Waller's song. Waller's song, entitled "Go, Lovely Rose," was written in five-line stanza forms.[39] It was set to music by Henry Lawes.

Envoi (1919), however, is independent of Waller and is a masterpiece of Pound. As a craftsman, Pound has tried to revive the lyric tradition in modern idiom, which he found missing in twentieth-century poetry. His interest in lyric was concerned with the vision of poetic excellence. The two great lyric traditions that he discovered before 1913, were the Melic and Provencal. The particular characteristic of melic and Provencal's lyric traditiosn is a unique combined effect of sound and tempo, which determines the volume of the sound movement of a poem. Moreover, in the tradition of free verse, it is easy to learn "the feel of thing" and the "candence."[40] The poem has melopoeic and logopoeic properties which, as explained by Pound, deal in force and attitude of mind respectively.[41] In this poem, there is singing quality.

The poem contains three stanzas. The very opening line of the first stanza, "Go, dumb-born book," is a variation on the popular song of Edmund Waller, "Go, lovely rose." The poet achieves objectivity through historical framework of Waller's time.[42] In the last stanza the contrast is between a cultural period and the culturally desert conditions of the present day England. The narrator, presents the song, in the contexts of Waller. The "culture of Waller" is seen missing in modern England, which represents the virtues of Lady Valentine. Therefore, the narrator in this poem bids good-bye to England because he feels that some other mouth "may be as fair as hers." The quest theme is again hinted at in this poem. The first section of the poem is a farewell to London, in a larger perspective.[43]

The second part of *Hugh Selwyn Mauberley* consists of only five poems. The first poem which opens the second section is entitled *Mauberley 1920*. The last poem of the first sequence is *Envoi (1919)*, which suggests preparation for farewell. The first poem of the second part thus marks Pound's final departure from London. The dates mentioned, 1919 and 1920 suggest this. Mauberley lives in his own glossy world of thoughts; and when he compares his vision of aestheticism with the prevalent chaotic conditions, he feels isolated. The character of Mauberley is not historical, but fictive and a type who has impressions and aesthetic feelings. The narrator criticizes the failure of the age; he condemns the external record of events. Mauberley fails badly as an artist whose perception is limited. Through him Pound attacks aestheticism and impressionism. The satirical mode brings a balance between the two sections which wipe off fragmentary assimilation of facts. The only change that takes place is the mode of condemnation.

Mauberley, 1920 is "an ironic self-contemplation of the aesthete-poet Mauberley. His inadequacies as an artist are treated in the four poems of this second sequence. Three of these echo, internally or in their titles, phrases from the poems of the first, more objective sequence."[44] The Ovidian epigraph of the poem *Vacuos exercet aera morsus* ("snaps at the empty air")[45] is ironically used. Jacquemart, a designer, is a reference from

Theophile Gautier.[46] Messalia was a Roman Empress, Penelope is the wife of Odysseus, and Flaubert is a prose writer. They stand for varied experience of life in art. The last stanza refers to two famous painters, Pier Francesca (really Piero della Francesca) and Pisanello, Vittore Pisano, a fourteenth century Veronese painter. Francesca's art was impersonal and colourless; Pisanello designed Greek coinage. "To forge Achia" refers to the Grecian art. Pisanello's art was an attempt at perfection. In the second stanza onwards Mauberley shows the limitation of his aestheticism. His art in profile lacked the colourfulness of Francesca and the skill of Pisanello. The irony is more clear: Mauberley is not competent to provide colour and shape to his profiles. His is the limited potentiality of an emgraver. He can not "forge Achaia." Nor does he have the precision of Flaubert; under his inspiration he attempts the "art in profile."

The speaker dissociates from serious art and gets interest in the study of a lady, an immoral woman, the Roman empress. The impotent Mauberley's interest in Messalina is satirical. He lacks the active passion of life. Ironic reference to the phallic and ambrosial, the sex symbolism of the third poem of the first section, is implied in the allusion to Messalina.

In the second sequence of poems the aesthetic view of the speaker is strongly ascertained with a kind of hedonistic vision in the epigraph of the second poem. The epigraph is from Caid Ali, and suggests Mauberley's assumptions about sex and art. It can be rendered in English as follows: "What do they know about love, and what they can understand? If they do not understand poetry and if they do not feel music, what can they understand of this passion in comparison to the rose which is cruel, or the perfume of violets and a thunder?" Mauberley understands none of these, and he is a failure as an artist and as a lover. Even though he feels the power of Venus and Eros, he fails to respond to it actively. The failure of the narrator is emotional. He reviews beauty in nostalgiacally. The poet again presents the Greek vision of beauty. The quest of beauty is persued, but it proves ineffective. The protagonist understands his loss which gives "narcissiastic satisfaction"[47] to his suppressed ego.

Mauberley's aestheticism loses its validity in the fascination of love. He records his experience of love. His passion works on two levels; one is aesthetic and concerns music and poetry; the other is love and sexual delight. Thus, the failure is also of dual nature—artistic and biological. Sex as a creative force is smothered by commercialism. The second poem of the second section consists of eight stanzas; and the use of heavy style provides a complicated texture to the poem. The narrator communicates his personal anger in a detached form. The first stanza begins with the ironic remark "For three years," like the opening line of the first poem of the first section, where he refers to his alienation and struggle to achieve "the sublime." The change, in this poem, is remarkable. He points out his involvement with the evil in music, and enjoyed its aesthetic delight for three years, which did not last for long. He says very poignantly:

> FOR three years, diabolus in the scale,
> He drank ambrosia,
> All passes, ANANGKE prevails,
> Came end, at last, to that Arcadia.
>
> He had moved amid her phantasmagoria,
> Amid her galaxies,
> NUKTIS 'AGALMA
>
> (*EPSP*, p. 199)

Mauberley makes us notice his experience of love through ANANGKE, which means necessity[48] and refers to Eros. The next reference is to Bion's phrase "NUKTIS" AGALMA VUKTOS," i.e. "jewel of blue night." When contrasted with the first reference Pound's reference gives an idea of the loss in love. Very sadly the speaker, who enjoyed the pleasures of the company of Aphrodite's loveliness in evening star (the phantos-gomeric world of miracles as stated by Lambert Strether in James' novel *The Ambassador*),[49] comes to feel his loss. The "Arcadia" is a reminiscence of the past experience. Mauberley elaborates the same sexual involvement in the next two stanzas. The broken speech rhythm shows the drift of the protagonist:

> Drifted...drifted precipitate,
> Asking time to be rid of...
> Of his bewilderment; to designate
> His new found orchid....
>
> (*EPSP*, p. 199)

Mauberley communicates how he drifted. He expresses his freedom from "bewilderment"—the Arcadia mentioned in the first stanza. The pun on the word "orchid" (i.e. *Iopxis,*[50] testicle) has yielded many interpretations. The orchid correlates to the "aerial flower"[51] and active love. The typographical sign between two words "drifted...drifted," in the second line and again in the fourth stanza "certain...certain..." distinguish the emotional intensity. His involvement, even at one stage, made him unable to separate "TO AGATHON," the good, from the "chaff." He was unable to make a distinction between passion and art. The scientific term "seismograph," an instrument that registers the earthquake, refers to the recording of the intensity of emotional disturbances caused by sexual weaknesses. The analogy shows the importance of sex in the context of ethical, moral, scientific and literary evaluation. Moreover, the "ecological totality"[52] of Gourmont fascinated Pound, and he accepted the philosophy of sex which perpetuates life. To Pound, sex also combines the forces of "tactile" and "magnetic" senses.[53] But the "fundamental passion" did not make the protagonist able to communicate his exact emotion. He remained amazed and inactive. He expresses his dejection and wrath in the phrase "biting empty air," the tone of the poem ridicules Mauberley.

The metamorphosed dogs[54] reveal the impotence, disgust and mental disorder of the protagonist. These dogs were left as "epilogues" to him. What a realization! The anguish, poignant feelings, inability of expressing his love, failure as an artist, and impotent sexual urge in a weak personality—these present the portrait of the defeated Mauberley.

The next poem is entitled "The Age Demanded," a quotation from the first sequence of poems. Mauberley contemplates his passivity, and the poem deals with shock and his failure. He gets penalty for his unrealistic realization of facts and feels a complete failure in the world.[55]

The first stanza deals with Mauberley's sensuous pre-occupation with love. Mauberley finds himself unfit. The next two lines present the sense of love—"red-beaked steeds of/ The Cytherean," a reference to the chariot of love drawn by the doves of Aphrodite. The self-indulgence in sensuousness confines Mauberley to a self-imposed world of thoughts. The "glow of porcelain" the "glaze," and "revery" keep him always aloof from social reality. His "gaze" is always baffled, and the reality appears to him in fitful glimpses. The passivity of the protagonist with regard to reality shows the tragic failure of the artist. The narrator, time and again, remembers his dreamy world. Beauty appears to him even via Shakespeare's sonnet 18.[56] But his partial perceptivity isolates him. Moreover the elimination of "The manifest universe" is not good for him. He gets once again involved with the impression of an earthly paradise. His inner blurring is:

> Nothing, in brief, but maudlin confession,
> Irresponse to human aggression,
> Amid the precipitation, down-float
> Of insubstantial manna,
> Lifting the faint susurrus
> Of his subjective hosannah.
>
> (*EPSP*, p. 202)

The poet uses "susurrus" and "hosannah," unusual expressions, point out the spiritually degenerate state. Biblical images are used for an ironic purpose. Mauberley meets his Exodus from men of letters, as he fails to make a contact with a "better tradition." But his integrity in the face of his so-called "betters", such as Nixon, saves him from the literary "doctrine of chances."

In the next poem, the narrator presents a fantasy. In order to escape the horror of literary London, the protagonist drifts to "scattered Moluccas." The Impressionist escapes to the South Seas. The poet projects his "tropical vision" and goes to find beauty in the travels of Flaubert and Carthage to Africa.[57] The tragedy occurs, and Mauberley betrays himself. The poet identifies him with Elpenor, who fell from the roof of Circe and spoke to Odysseus in Canto I:

> "A man of no fortune, and with a name to come.
> And set my oar up, that I swung mid fellows."[58]

The fate of Mauberley compels him to meet his end:

> "I was
> And I no more exist;
> Here drifted
> An hedonist."
>
> (*EPSP*, p. 203)

The passivity of the protagonist leads him to no conclusion. The epitaph at the burial place of Mauberley connects the poem with the first in the first sequence: a man of "no fortune, and with a name to come" reminds the burial in *E.P. Ode Pour L'Election De Son Sepulchre.* How ironic is the fact that the artist who has been a failure, perpetuates himself in these lines, he drifts a "hedonist."

The last poem is *Medallion,* the final poem of the second section like *Envoi (1919)* of the first sequence. It is a masterpiece in etching out the beauty and artistic grandeur embodied in a woman. The portrait presents a singing lady. It is a short poem consisting of only four stanzas. The first two stanzas present two portraits. The first is the portrait of La Columbina by a medieval artist Bernadino Luini.[59] The second portrait recaptures the "Head of Aphrodite."[60] The third stanza deals with a combined effect of the details of the first two stanzas. The beauty is, again, like porcelain gaze. Though willing to portray a perfect lady, the narrator projects her eyes, and glazy oval face:

The face-oval beneath the glaze,
Bright in its suave bounding-line, as,
Beneath half-watt rays,
The eyes turn topaz.

(*EPSP*, p. 204)

Medallion shows a moral tone. It contains a final irony.[61] The passive Mauberley, and the aesthete in him, suffers from a limited vision of art; and he perceives beauty in the tradition of the past, in cultural references. But as an artist Mauberley achieves the chiseled art of Gautier's art of presentation.

Hugh Selwyn Mauberley is a great poem written in the ironical mode. Pound has thrown his whole weight on the process of creation. It is an effective satire on the culture, social ethos, and artistic collapse of London during the early 1920s. The poem is a tragedy in the sense that it deals with the sad plight of an artist, with a glossy world of impressionism and aesthetic notions of art in a callous commercialized world. Mauberley, the protagonist meets with his tragic destiny; and yet, in another sense, the poem is a comedy, too. The comic irony and satire of the poem are directed towards the literary establishment, the tendencies of the age, commercialism, and what "the age demanded."

The narrator, in the first section of the poem, confronts the pretentious, false, and artificial norms of the time. The literary period dealt with in the poem had its own superficial standards of taste and bourgeois demands. The narrator attacks these falsities and superficialities. But the aestheticism of the sincere artist does not seem to have been spared either. When the narrator turns his gaze inwards, he becomes self-depreciative. The tone of the poem betrays the narrator's self-criticism and his inadequacy, as an aesthete and lover of past beauty, to deal fully with the sordid present and to give us an adequate sense of *l'histoire contemporaine*.

But the poem as a whole is larger than the dramatized consciousness of the narrator, and it marks the line of departure in the development of Pound's own poetry. It is a farewell not so much to London, as superficially it seems to be, as to the aesthetic mode in which Pound had been writing his early lyrics. Henceforth, after burying the aesthete in him (yet who can bury him?), he would take to a more vigorous, vitriolic, and ironic mode which will give us an adequate sense of *l'histoira contemporaine.*

The poem is often considered to be a kind of condensed Jamesian Novel.[62] The early twentieth century period makes an unobtrusive incursion, by means of manifold voices, into the framework of *Hugh Selwyn Mauberley.* There are, in the poem, references, allusions, translations, persons, and adaptations which bring alien sensibilities and a kind of historical method of objective creation and criticism of prevailing conditions. The persona of the poet and Mauberley are ironically placed in hostile situations. This gives a sense of dramatic immediacy. The poem, on the whole, is an imaginative study of characters that are essentially real. Rupert Brooke, Gladstone, Swinburne, Buchanan, Dowson, Monsieur Verog Johnson, Brennbaum, Mr. Nixon, Robertson Nicoll, Lady Valentine, and others are all caught in their essence and they appear to contrast with one another.

The poem also belongs to a mode which Pound calls the art of "criticism in new composition."[63] This is the mode in which *Homage to Sextus Propertius* is also written.[64]

Hugh Selwyn Mauberley, as whole, is remarkable for his power of Logopoeia to use his own term for diction. In Pound's Logopoeia, there is no place for bad rhetoric. Generally, three kinds of verbal allusions are used to render the criticism of a milieu in poetry: overt, oblique, and the ironic. Throughout, in this poem, Pound uses overt allusions by way of personal names. This helps intellectual compression of meaning. Pound's logopoeia is charged with the reverberations of ironic stances. The poem begins with "ironically self-diminished portrait of Pound in the first section," and there is "a devastating portrait of Mauberley in the second sequence."[65]

The sense of the loss makes the poem's tone somewhat elegiac. The "ode" of the first sequence is a correlation of epical design; it begins *in media res.* The narrator's quest for beauty and art ends with the vision. The poem reverberates with irony and satire, and yet it is more than a satirical work. The protagonist diagnoses the ailing condition of the age, and provides the "art of cure" in the "cult of beauty" in both the end-sequence poems of *Hugh Selwyn Mauberley.*[66] The poem presents a unified vision of the protagonist and is a manifesto of art and beauty. It is Pound's first great triumph in the art of writing a long poem that is virtually a miniature epic, like some of his Cantos.

REFERENCES

1. F.R. Leavis, *New Bearings in English Poetry* (Harmondsworth: Penguin Books, 1963), p. 124.
2. *Ezra Pound: The Critical Heritage,* ed. Eric Homberger (London: Routledge and Kegan Paul, 1972), pp. 144-45.
3. R.P. Blackmur, *Form and Value in Modern Poetry* (Carden City: Doubleday, 1957), pp. 84-85.
4. T.S. Eliot, "Introduction," *Ezra Pound: Selected Poems* (London: Faber and Faber, 1948), p. 20.
5. Quoted by John J. Espey in *Ezra Pound: A Study in Composition* (Berkeley: University of California Press, 1955), p. 33.
6. Hugh Kenner, *The Poetry of Ezra Pound* (London: Faber and Faber, 1951), p. 173.
7. Richard A. Long, *The Explictor Encyclopaedia Modern Poetry,* Volume I, (June 1952), p. 231.
8. John J. Espey, *Ezra Pound's Mauberley: A Study in Composition,* p. 19.
9. "For we know all the things that have been in Troy", quoted by Lillian Feder in *Ancient Myth in Modern Poetry* (Princeton, New Jersey: Princeton University Press, 1971), p. 100.
10. *Ezra Pound: Selected Poems,* ed. T.S. Eliot (London: Faber and Faber, 1928), p. 173. Hereafter this source will be abbreviated to EPSP.
11. A.C. Partridge, *The Language of Modern Poetry* (London: Andre Deutsch Ltd., 1976), p. 51.
12. *Ezra Pound Selected Prose, 1909-65,* ed. William Cookson (London: Faber and Faber, 1973), p. 55.

13. Monroe K. Spears, *Dionysus and the City: Modernism in Twentieth-Century Poetry* (London: Oxford University Press, 1971), p. 51.
14. G.S. Fraser, *Ezra Pound* (Edinburgh: Oliver and Boyd, 1962), p. 57.
15. K.K. Ruthven, *A Guide to Ezra Pound's Personae, 1926.* (Berkeley: University of California Press, 1969), p. 131.
16. "What man, What hero, What God" — Pindar, *Olympian Odes,* II, 2.
17. *The Selected Letters of Ezra Pound, 1907-41,* ed. D.D. Paige (London: Faber & Faber, 1971), p. 91.
18. J.P. Sullivan, "Ezra Pound and the Classics," *New Approaches to Ezra Pound,* ed. Eva Hesse (London: Faber and Faber, 1969), pp. 219-20.
19. Quoted in K.K. Ruthven, *A Guide to Ezra Pound's Personae (1926)* (Berkeley: University of California Press, 1969), p. 58.
20. *The Selected Letters,* ed. D.D. Paige, p. 180.
21. Ezra Pound, "M. Antonius Flamininus and John Keats: A Kinship in Genius," *Book News Monthly,* XXVI, 6 (February, 1908), p. 466.
22. K.K. Ruthven, *A Guide to Ezra Pound's Personae (1926),* p. 135.
23. Quoted in Williams V; Sparos, "The Modulating Voice of High Selwyn Mauberley," *Wiscousin Studies in Comtemporary Literature,* VI, 1 (Winter-Spring, 1965), p. 90.
24. K.K. Ruthven, *A Guide to Ezra Pound's Personae (1926)* p. 135.
25. F.R. Leavis, *New Bearings in English Poetry* (Harmondsworth: Penguine Books, 1963), p. 121.
26. A.L. French, "Olympian Aparthein": Pound's Hugh *Helyn Mauberley* and *Modern Poetry*", Ezra Pound, ed. J.P. Sullivan (Harmondsworth: Penguin Books, 1970, p. 336.
27. K.K. Ruthven, *A Guide to Ezra Pound's Personae 1926,* pp. 136-37.
28. *Ibid.,* p. 138.
29. G.S. Fraser, *Ezra Pound* (Edinburgh: Oliver and Boyd Ltd., 1962), p. 57.
30. *Ibid.,* p. 58.
31. Quoted in K.K. Ruthven, *A Guide to Ezra Pound's Personae 1926,* p. 139.
32. Charles Norman, *Ezra Pound* (London: Macdonald, 1969), p. 220.
33. *The Selected Letters of Ezra Pound,* ed. D.D. Paige, p. 21.
34. K.K. Ruthven, *A Guide to Ezra Pound's Personae 1926,* p. 139.
35. Richard Sieburth, *Instigations, Ezra Pound and Remy de Gourmont* (Cambridge, Mass.: Harvard University Press, 1978), pp. 143.-44.

36. Quoted in John J. Espey, *Ezra Pound's Mauberley: A Study in Composition* (Berkeley: University of California Press, 1955), p. 31.
37. K.K. Ruthven, *A Guide to Ezra Pound's Personae 1926*, p. 140.
38. Herbert N. Schneidau, *Ezra Pound: The Image nd the Real* (Baton Rouge: Louisiana State University Press, 1969), ›. 163.
39. Charles Norman, *Ezra Pound*, pp. 223-24.
40. *Literary Essays*, p. 93.
41. *Ibid.*, pp. 25-26.
42. George Dekker, *Sailing After Knowledge: The Cantos of Ezra Pound, A Critical Appraisal* (New York: Barnes & Noble, 1963), p. 158.
43. Thomas E. Connolly, *Accent, A Quarterly of New Literature* (1956), 65.
44. Walter Sutton, *American Free Verse: The Modern Revolution in Poetry* (New York: A New Directions Book, 1973), p. 59.
45. Quoted in K.K. Ruthven, *A Guide to Ezra Pound's Personae 1926*, p. 141.
46. *Ibid.*, p. 142.
47. Lillian Feder, *Ancient Myth in Modern Poetry* (Princeton: Princeton University Press, 1971), p. 102.
48. K.K. Ruthven, *A Guide to Ezra Pound's Personae 1926*, p. 143.
49. *Ibid.*, p. 143
50. *Ibid.*, p. 144.
51. John J. Espey, *Ezra Pound's Mauberley: A Study in Composition*, p. 51.
52. Richard Sieburth, *Instigations: Ezra Pound and Remy de Gourmont*, p. 134.
53. *Literary Essays*, p. 341.
54. *The Metamorphosis of Ovid*, trans. Mary M. Innes (Harmondsworth: Penguin Books, 1955), p. 177.
55. F.R. Leavis, *New Bearings in English Poetry*, p. 125.
56. A. French, "Olympian Apathein": Pound's *Hugh Selwyn Mauberley and Modern Poetry*," *Ezra Pound*, ed. J.P. Sullivan (Harmondsworth: Penguin Books, 1970), p. 340.
57. Quoted in John J. Espey, *Ezra Pound's Mauberley: A Study in Composition*, p. 39.
58. Ezra Pound, *A Draft of XXX Cantos* (London: Faber and Faber, 1930).
59. K.K. Ruthven, *A Guide to Ezra Pound's Personae 1926*, p. 126.
60. *Ibid.*, p. 146.

61. Hugh Kenner, "*Mauberley*", *Ezra Pound a Collection of Critical Essays*, ed. Walter Sutton (Englewood Cliffs: Prentice-Hall, Inc., 1963), p. 55.
62. *The Selected Letters of Ezra Pound*, ed. D.D. Paige, p. 180.
63. *Literary Essays*, p. 75.
64. Hugh Witemeyer, *The Poetry of Ezra Pound: Forms and Renewal 1908-20* (Berkeley: University of California Press, 1969), p. 14.
65. Christine Brooke-Rose, *A ZBC of Ezra Pound* (London: Faber and Faber, 1971), p. 159.
66. Hugh Witemeyer, *The Poetry of Ezra Pound: Forms and Renewal 1908-20*, p. 163.

6

The Cantos: Digging Out of the Vital Spots

A Draft of XXX Cantos (1930) explored a new type of form, but the critics were unable to discover any unified scheme in it. Pound continued to work on his scheme and by 1970 he had published 117 Cantos. They are his masterpiece poems which demonstrate his preoccupation with great design and project. *A Draft of XXX Cantos* is a long poem distinct from his earlier poems on the one hand and from his later Cantos on the other. Pound has started writing his Cantos as early as 1917.

A study of *A Draft of XXX Cantos* involves Pound's poetic world and his mind and sensibility. The "draft" in the title indicates the poet's intention to extend it as a much longer poem. But the Cantos which appeared in parts with different titles can be studied separately. The first thirty Cantos, in this manner, belong to the first large segment of the whole work which appeared in the book form in 1920.

Pound published his *first three Cantos* in *Poetry* in 1916. The fourth Canto was published in the *Dial* in 1920, and the *Criterion* brought out Malatesta Cantos, IX-XII, in 1923. The *Dial* published, in the summer issue of 1925, Cantos XVII-XIX. These Cantos were written along with *Hugh Selwyn Mauberley* and *Homage to Sextus Propertius*. But the appearance of *A Draft of XVI Cantos* (1925) met with an unfavourable response. Mr. Glenway Wescott reviewed the collection and underestimated its importance:

> From time to time a canto, like a block of cumbersome, streaked marble, has appeared in one of the few brave

> magazines, as if on a pedestal of temporary stucco and obscured by scaffolding.... The structure of the individual cantos is too subtle to be enjoyed; or perhaps there is no structure, perhaps this is a rag-bag like Sordello....[1]

The criticism pointed out the fact that the first draft of XVI Cantos was lacking consistency. And after five years, the appearance of *A Draft of XXX Cantos* also looked terse and textually complicated for interpretation. Eda Lou Walton in this poem discovered many types of complexities. Pound's use of allusion, references, mythic characters and quotations seemed to him a meaningless documentation. He considered it only "an intellectual game."[2] Geoffrey Grigson went a step ahead and made a downward swoop on Pound with his severe criticism. His main complaint was that the poem did not contain any growth. It appeared lacking the "compulsive and pervading discipline."[3] There was a demand of footnotes in order to make the poem intelligible.

In the context of the use of music, values, philosophy, language and history, many treated the XXX Cantos as a non-serious poem. After these reviewers, came a flock of established scholars who assessed the poem negatively. The poem looked to them as a mere demonstration of facts which adhered to a kind of disconnected documentation and illogical association of ideas. Most of the criticism that has appeared is prominently concerned with fault finding business. The Cantos, thus, still suffer from the negative criticism of George Dekker, Rosenthal, Noel Stock, Michael Alaxander, A. Alvarez, George P. Eliot, Theodor Weiss and Richard Peever. Their criticism seems to be a kind of conspiracy against the proper recognition of the Cantos.

There are, however, a few critics who have tried to evaluate the Cantos sympathetically. They have made efforts to find out a unifying pattern and relevant things in the poem. Some of them are Hugh Kenner, Lewis Leary and Clark Emery, and Daniel D. Pearlman. Hugh Kenner has presented a brilliant analysis of Pound's poetry and his technique. He deals with the striking salient features of Cantos and tries to establish unity of the poem in a structural context. He brilliantly remarks:

> Pound, quite consciously, never thinks of using two motifs, two blocks of rendering, except as parts, integral parts, of a larger rhythm of juxtaposition and recurrence. This balancing and recurrence of motifs is what holds together single cantos. It also holds together the entire work, the temporarily unfinished condition of which doesn't diminish the structural solidity of the portion existing, any more than the absence of a roof diminishes the inter-relation of proportions among cathedral arches.[5]

Hugh Kenner finds out certain recurring things and rhythms of recurrence as well, which, in his opinion, provide a major form to Pound's Cantos. But the thematic development of the poem on the accepted pattern of theme repetition does not qualify the demand of unity. His criticism seems to be unconvincing. Another famous critic whose sympathetic criticism is a good study of Pound's Cantos, is Daniel Pearlman. Mr. Pearlman has presented an intensive study of Pound's total Cantos in the context of the study of Time. He makes efforts to find a correlation between thesis, antithesis, and synthesis. Time, according to him, appears as a major subject in Pound's Cantos which gathers all sorts of episodes, facts, events and historical elaborations. He studies the total Cantos of Ezra Pound in the context of disorder, order and love which bring a parallel division of Inferno, Purgatorio, and Paradiso. Moreover, he seems to be interested in the analysis of the Cantos dealing with time-consciousness.[6] But the criticism of Pearlman presents only one aspect of Pound's treatment of his major work. Every poem involves the consciousness of time factor. The clear-cut division of Inferno, Purgatorio and Paradiso, as found in Dante's *Divine Comedy*, would be confining the poem to the sole study of one aspect of the major form of the Cantos.

The Cantos are encyclopaedic. They possess the form of a miniature epic. They present several cycles of experiences. The mode of the poem is ironical. Pound, in order to establish truth, presents two kinds of values which are juxtaposed with each other. The contrast, thus, posits a kind of criticism which is elucidated with facts, personae, allusions and quotations in the ironic mode. The poem, thus, grows like a tree and internally several things are directed to some broad outlines of the major design of the poem.

Pound discards the idea of a systematic growth of plot and detest the conventional theory of Aristotelian beginning, middle and end. Because there are many examples of "very important chunks of world-literature in which form, major form, is remarkable mainly for absence."[7] His concept of an epic is a poem that contains history.[8] About the form, he remarks:

> I think there is a 'fluid' as well as a 'solid' content, that some poems may have form as a tree has form, some as water poured into a vase. That most symmetrical forms have certain uses. That a vast number of subjects cannot be precisely, and therefore not properly rendered in symmetrical forms.[9]

Pound's Cantos, thus, literally survey the development of human civilization and different cultures with their downfall and grandeur in a larger perspective. The Cantos of Ezra Pound can be studied as an epical poem from two angles. The first is in the context of his own concept of epic containing history and the second belongs to his device of condensation.

There is controversy about the epical design of the poem; several explanations have been given by the author himself and some of his critics dealing with the scheme of the poem. Pound wrote in a letter to his father Homer Pound, in which he mentions the outlines of the poem:

> Dear Dad:--/--/ Afraid the whole damn poem is rather obscure, especially in fragments. Have I ever given you outline of main scheme::: or whatever it is?
>
> I. Rather like, or unlike subject and response and counter subject in fugue.
>
> A.A. Live man goes down into world of Dead
>
> C.B. The "repeat in history"
>
> B.C. The "magic moment" or moment of metamorphosis, bust thru fro quotidien into "divine or permanent world." Gods, etc. ....
>
> Various things keep cropping up in the poem. The original world of gods; the Trojan war, Helen on the wall of Troy with

> the old men fed up with the whole show and suggesting she be sent back of Greece.[10]

Ezra Pound's letter shows his concern with history, myth and modern civilization. Myth appears to him a timeless history. The scheme as cited above suggests three planes of values. The first division mentioned as A.A. refers to Homeric world. The second, C.B., points out the treatment of history which discovers the ordeals of the past. The third division belongs to the world of myth and metamorphosis. Myth presents gods and goddesses as archetype of human beings. Metamorphosis conveys the transformational values. History deals with disorder and chaos. The theme of the journey of *The Divine Comedy* of Dante is to Pound a kind of experience. The method of description of the discovery of experience is more or less an elastic method of presentation. The second explanation which is concerned with the controversy of the design of poem is a triplex analogy of experience described by W.B. Yeats. Pound offered some geometrical designs as the scheme of his first 27 Cantos, which Yeats mentions:

> ...I cannot find any adequate definition—A B C D and then JKLM, and then each set of letters repeated, and then A B C D inverted and this repeated, and then a new element X Y Z, then certain letters that never recur, and then all sorts of combinations of X Y Z and J K L M and A B C D and D C B A, and all set whirling together. He has shown me upon the wall a photograph of a Cosimo Tura decoration in three compartments, in the upper the Triumph of Love and the Triumph of Chastity, in the middle Zodiacal signs, and in the lower certain events in Cosimo Tura's day. The Descent and the Metamorphosis—A B C D and J K L M—his fixed elements, took the place of the Zodiac, the archetypal persons—X Y Z—that of the Triumphs, and certain modern events—his letters that do not recur—that of those events in Cosimo Tura's day.[11]

The outlines seemingly do not solve the problem of structure of the Cantos. Nonetheless the close study of Yeatsian analogy focuses upon the nature of the mode of experiences. The entire geometrical design deals with the frescoes of Francesco del Cossa in the Palazzo Schifanoia in Ferrara. The pictures were painted in three parallel strips. The revelation of these strips are analogous to three values. Pound pointed out the justification of frescoes to Hayden Carruth that the top strip modeled on Petrarch's *Trionfi*, presented allegorical values which are permanent; and the middle strip dealing with stars (sign of Zodiac), planets and cosmology is like recurring themes of history—quest, love, discoveries etc., and the last, lowest strip refers to actual life of Borso d'Este (1413-17), Duke of Ferrara.[12] Despite this interpretation, three themes appear as the permanent, the recurrent, and the casual which were thought as the best divisions of the Cantos.[13]

Despite the fresco analogy, there appears a psychological pattern. Psychologically, three types of experience express hate, comprehension, and worship, which formulate the feelings of Inferno, Purgatory and Paradise. The psychological analogy also provides a mode of experience. Dante's *The Divine Comedy* was a journey through the states of mind:

> The journey of the vision begins in a thick forest midway along life's road, whence Dante, in fear of certain symbolical beasts, is led by Virgil through and out of Hell, and to the summit of Purgatory, where another guide awaits to accompany him out through the concentric spheres of the heavens into unbounded heaven above them.[14]

Pound took interest in Dante for many reasons. He treated Dante as a great poet like Homer, Chaucer, and Shakespeare, who were poets of consciousness. Dante showed his awareness of the inner world. His vision deals with an inward journey. Dante had the consciousness of "the spaces of mind, its reach and its perspective."[15]

The triplex analogy as that of Dante, the fresco theory of Yeats, and the three-phase value of Pound all deal with modes of experience. They narrate the story of a culture. The method of presentation of facts and ideas belong to the method of expedition which summarises values in Joycean style. The Cantos can be grouped together, in the context of corresponding themes. The first group of sixteen poems has a pattern in which the movement of time, scales between Homer and the first world war, and 'factive personalities' like Sigismundo Malatesta,

Sordello and El Cid appear as symbol of values; and the group ends with the vision of a hell that presents modern usurers, profiteers, businessmen, journalists, and bankers. The end of the first sixteen Cantos take out the protagonist of the poem out of the Inferno. The pattern of this group, as Walter Sutton says, also belong to Dantean structure of "hell-purgatory-heaven."[16] The rest of the Cantos can be divided on the basis of the nature of values, in five groups, in which a sequence may be seen.

The first three Cantos present history. They approach the growth of the rest of the Cantos. In Canto IV to Canto VII, the poet shows his phantastikan. They present realities in glimpses. Malatesta group of Cantos run from Cantos VIII to XI. In these Cantos the Renaissance appears with its historical grandeur. The next two Cantos, XII and XIII, present moral examples. The Hell group deals with from XIV to Canto XVI. In this way five groups appear in the first sixteen Cantos.[17]

The next fourteen Cantos, again deal with the history of the Renaissance period and modern commercial values. The XVII Canto repeats the approach with magnificent historical overlayings of Italian and Greek cultures. Cantos XVIII and XXI deal with sabotage, war and revolution. Canto XX presents lotus eaters. The Canto is a depiction of lyric tradition. In next three Cantos, XXI to XXIII, confusion and order are brought together. In Canto XXIV to XXVI, Venice is portrayed with its history of rise and fall. The Cantos XXVII and XXVIII repeat the metamorphic values again. They present mythical experience of human life. Canto XXIX is concerned with Helen. The female beauty is portrayed. The last Canto XXX presents the modern civilization.[18] It is a final tableau which presents all sorts of values of time. The thirty Cantos, in short, seem to be a palette, on which different colours are mixed.

They present a broad spectrum of mythical, historical and modern values of human race. The poem presents an Inferno at large: Purgatorio appears in Canto XVII; and Paradiso in Canto XX. The protagonist passes through the dark forest of the decline of history and makes a continuous search for order.

The quest theme in history gives the poem an encyclopaedic design; the poem is discontinuous in form. The poem contains a vast panorama of history. T.S. Eliot, felt the greatness of Pound's Cantos as they contained some philosophy of Pound, but appreciated the manner in which his ideas were expressed.[19]

The Cantos are important, no doubt, for their encyclopaedic treatment of subjects. But the first XXX Cantos show its supremacy as Pound's poetic techniques are employed. It is a study of structure which denies the existence of any kind of poetic logic found even in the most modern poets like Olson and Duncan.[20] But the theme of journey is pursued as a continuous effort of arresting moments of history. The encyclopaedic form does not present religious values as that of Dante's epic poem. Nonetheless the theme of journey, always can be a great subject for a long poem, in any period and "episodic theme is perhaps best described as the theme of the boundary of consciousness."[21] The broad framework of encyclopaedic form has been changing from period to period. In ironic age, which means the modern age, the poet is more concerned with his art, and the vision. The experiences that the poet transcends, come from the vastness of history. History with changing course of civilization and flashes of moments, confronts a negative order. Hence the mode of presentation becomes ironical and discontinuous. In this way, as Cantos deal with history of human race, they become epical. In this context Fry aptly remarks:

> So the ironic mode is rationalized by critical theories of the essential discontinuity of poetry. The paradoxical technique of the poetry which is encyclopaedic and yet discontinuous, the technique of *The Waste Land* and of Ezra Pound's *Cantos,* is, like its direct opposite in Wordsworth, a technical innovation heralding a new mode.[22]

In short, *A Draft of XXX Cantos,* is a modern epic poem in encyclopaedic form. It deals with the Western culture and themes of disorder which are unrolled by history. Greek, Italy, Renaissance, and contemporary Europe appear with their episodes and events. The poem apparently seems to be a combination of continuous and discontinuous form with autobiographical and objective details and facts of history. The persona of each Canto shifts its position and merges into the persona of the protagonist of the poem according to the need of the point of view. The Cantos in short present an authentic criticism of the Western culture.

The first Canto begins with Homeric Scaffold. It is a translation of the Odyssey, Book XI, into a Latin version of Homer rendered by Andreas Divus in 1538. Pound's adaptation of Latin from Homer's Greek is significant. It makes the best use of a living language of the Renaissance period. The very translation is a recreation of the antiquated language. The Canto begins with the theme of Nekuia passage. The poem presents the world of spirits. The hero makes a journey to the dead land, full of shades and ghosts. Homer's hero is Pound's persona who brings out an enormous world of experience which deals with the theme of "descent into Hades."

Odysseus after a long separation from his wife, Penelope and son Telemachus, goes back home. His journey is backward. He faces hardships, and visits the underworld. The theme of nostos, literally is a kind of quest too. The wandering hero is led by Circe. Circe as an enchantress changed Odysseus' men into swine. But she failed to transform Odysseus who willingly spent one year with her. The hero of the poem is Pound's persona who experiences pain and suffering, and educates himself to live again with the living men. The experience gained by Pound-Odysseus is of many types; Odysseus shares the suffering of his relatives, of his friend Elpenor and other ghosts, through his own metamorphosis. Pound's persona through Homeric world, gains some knowledge which seems to be unattainable and in the end, the Canto ends with the vision of beauty in Aphrodite that appears as a source of creative power. Odysseus is an intellectual wanderer. He passes through many phases of life, gets a new vision. Tiresias, a mythological character is his friend who makes many prophecies. Odysseus's return to Ithaca, for Pound, is a backward journey to deep rooted European civilization.

What was the necessity of Odyssean type of discovery? Why did Pound not adopt *Iliad* as his framework which provides a larger scaffold of epic pattern? Homer's Odysseus makes his journey in a nostalgic context which gives the impression of the effect of tragic mode; and nostalgia is fit for tragic ethos, not for epic.[23] If Pound wanted to begin the Cantos in epic mode, he should have preferred some different model. Such vague criticism is easily answerable. The voyage theme is based on the *Odyssey*, which is a metaphor to Pound, who uses the term "Nekuia" which opens to him the book of racial history. Pound himself is a guide in the journey of mysterious world and the measuring instrument of his experience is not Aquina's map but "periplum," which not only records events of journey, but also presents a selective view of history. Pound defined his searching method:

> Periplum, not as land looks on a map
> But as sea bord seen by men sailing.
>
> (Canto LIX)

The sense of journey may be nostalgic, but the Homeric poem belongs to the form of "epic of Return." Like other epics, Homer's *Odyssey* also deals with cyclical action, like the Iliad and Aeneid. Frye finds in these epics a "kind of nadir of the total cyclical action."[24] Moreover it is the *Iliad* that is tragic. The *Odyssey* offers to Pound a theme of great discovery which frustrates the optimism of a man. But it ends with a belief. Similarly, the theme of *The Divine Comedy* expresses also a mode of journey through different regions. Pound has combined Homeric and Dantean theme into one. The Canto I begins with Odyssean adventure which also describes the strong individuality of the poet's character. The strong individual characteristic is the main quality of all factive personalities in the Cantos.

The poem is a translation of a Latin version into English. Pound discovered Andreas Divus in 1906, and made the Nekuia, his own journey to Europe. He mentions the date 1538. Homer's period becomes contemporary of Divus. The XXX Cantos end with "Pope" who almost belonged to the same time. Moreover,

Pound rendered Anglo-Saxon rhythm. Divus' Latin provided him "poetic motion"; and "swing and mood of the subject."[25] The opening lines demonstrate the artistic use of sound and pause:

> And then went down to the ship,
> Set keel to breakers, forth on the godly sea, and
> We set up mast and sail on that swart ship,
> Bore sheep aboard her, and our bodies also
> Heavy with weeping, and winds from sternward
> Bore us out onward with bellying canvas,
> Circe's this craft, the trim-coifed goddess.[26]

Pound revives the rhythm of his own poem, *Seafarer,* in Anglo-Saxon verse, that bristled with sound and rhythm of old English. Ezra Pound has enlivened the Renaissance language in this translation and made it a living language.

The Canto, on the whole, presents the mood and emotional depth of the original poem. The Greek language presents emotions with audible and visual description; and the Latin of Renaissance, particularly of Andreas Divus gives insight to Pound to use interior monologue and modern idiom of present day English. The Canto as translation of Nekuia passage investigates different roots of cultures. The translation presents the source and its functional value, as Hugh Kenner has noted:

> And Canto I (as it eventually became), with its thudding alliteration, its Saxon vocables (*swart, mead, dreory*), its Anglo-Norman compounds (*sea-bord, trim-coifed*), its Greek survivals (*pyre, Kimmerian*), its prevalent monosyllables ("And we set up mast and sail on that swart ship"), its Homeric narrative and its injunction to Divus, recapitulates the story of a pattern persisting undeformable while many languages have flowed through it and many more pronunciations in the thousands of years it has been a property of the Western mind.[27]

The narrative technique that Pound took from Divus' Homer presents the vast world of experience. The Canto brings out an exhibition of aesthetic and sexual world. The aestheticism is explained through the myth of Odysseus, gods and goddesses; and the sexual experience is promoted by ghosts, and crewmen. The enchantress Circe perverts sexually infatuated characters and turns them into swine. The speaker of the poem in first person narrates his experience and his contact with souls. "I" is identified with Odysseus who is used by the poet as his own mask. Odysseus as the protagonist of the Canto knows everything, feels everything and sees everything. He is an explorer, quester, adventurer and stands for order.

The first part of the Canto deals with the Mediterranean scene. The natural surrounding of sea-side, and unfavourable winds blowing against sails are presented with Circe's magical effect in the nature. The "Kimmerian lands" looks beautiful with "closed-webbed mist" and "Swartest night." The ideogrammatic presentation, like cinematographic details, presents different portraits of nature. The blood offering-scene and shades speaking to Odysseus present a lovely scene:

> These many crowded about me; with shouting,
> Pallor upon me, cried to my men for more beasts;
> Slaughtered the herds, sheep slain of bronze;
> Poured ointment, cried to the gods,
> To Pluto the strong, and praised Proserpine;
> Unsheathed the narrow sword,
> I sat to keep off the impetuous impotent dead,
> Till I should hear Tiresias.
>
> (*EZRA POUND The Cantos*, p. 4)

Ghosts appear one after another. Elpenor speaks to Odysseus, Anticlea also speaks; and, in the end, Aphrodite appears with her "Golden crown." The poem ends with "so that." The beginning with "And" and the end with "so that" mark the epical design of the Cantos. The first Canto contains speech rhythm. It is almost written in phrases, which are monologues. Pound uses dramatic monologues in speeches of the ancient characters who present "modern consciousness."[28] The sentences in this poem are in small units which help in removing the dullness. Elliptical expressions are masterly. In this Canto the poet presents the technique of translation, handling of persona, historiography of Greek and the mythical mode of antiquity, which operate in all the Cantos.

The second Canto begins with metamorphosis; the tale is concerned with pirates who wanted to sell a young boy. But Bacchus saved him and turned those sailors into fish. The story has been adapted from Ovid's *Metamorphoses*. In *Metamorphoses* stories are concerned with characters who change into other forms. Pound uses these stories to record the emotional situation, as their themes project negative and positive values respectively. The Ovidian framework, in short, equates emotions with transformation episodes of gods and goddesses. The metamorphosis also recurs in Pound's style as changes are made in pronouns. The "I" or "my" in the Cantos are mythical characters, whom Pound lends his voice. Pound changed the Provencal stories into Ovidian tale of Procne and Philomela.[29]

The narrator presents Bacchus, who was the son of Jupiter and Semele. He is the god of wine. The archetypal characters like Helen, Eleanor, Tyro, and Dionysus are presented from different sources as *Mabinogion*, Fenollosa, Aeschylus, *Odyssey* XI and Remy de Gourmount. They present a cycle of history; they repeat themselves and metamorphose into one another. Gods and historical characters are brought together, where experiences are established at human level. Even persons of contemporary world, in later Cantos, are identified with such archetypal characters. Gods become human and factive personalities of history appear as divine beings. The second Canto opens with Browning's Sordello. The persona of Browning, Sordello from *The Ring and the Book,* becomes obviously Poundian. The reference of Sordello in Canto II belongs to many versions. But Sordello mentioned in the Canto is a historical figure. His story of love is concerned with Cunizza da Romano, wife of the Count Ricciardo di San Bonifazzio.[30] Browning wrote his 'Sordello' and he presented him as an intelligent man.

So-shu, a Chinese mythological character, and eyes of Picasso, present an abstraction of beauty. The poem, as it progresses, presents three parallel visions from the beginning to the end. The first comes from the *Iliad,* Book III. In this episode Priam is asked to send Helen back. The second vision is from

Ovid's *Metamorphoses,* in which the god Dionysus is kidnapped by the sailors who are, later, turned into animals. The third episode is concerned with the metamorphosis of the sea-nymph Ileuthyeria into coral. She saves herself from seduction. Daphne-Apollo mythical exposition opens its transformational world. These episodes bring great changes.[31] Helen with her destructive force is portrayed:

> 'Eleanor, elenaus and eleptolis!'
>   And poor old Homer blind, blind, as a bat,
> Ear, ear for the sea surge, murmur of old men's voices:
> 'Let her go back to the ships,
> Back among Grecian faces, lest evil come in our own,
> Evil and further evil and a curse cursed on our-children,
>
> (*EZRA POUND The Cantos,* p. 6)

Helen's description is borrowed from Aeschylus' *Agamemnon,* in which Helen is called "ship-destroying, man destroying and city destroying." The Aeschylus-Homer analogy, portrays a horrible woman whose beauty seems to destroy even the creative vision of Homer.[32]

The narrator continues his quest of experience. He meets the sea-god, and the young boy, standing with the narrator and the captain of the ship together. For little money, sailors wanted to sell him as a slave. The boy was none but god Dionysus. The metamorphosis that took place in the ship shows its relevance. Not only were the men changed into animals, but the atmosphere also underwent a great metamorphosis. "The sky overshot, dry with no tempest" expresses the unnatural view of the sea-side. The change in nature denotes the violation of order. The poet uses myth at this point to create awe and fear. This metamorphosis is caused by greed. Pound takes up "usura" as a clue for suffering and unnatural events. The action in the poem brings a kind of reversal of order. The whole presentation is a connotation of disorder—and negation. The transformation of men into beasts, witnesses the change in natural world—"Lifeless air become sinewed."

After the Greek episode comes Aphrodite, who appears as a vision of order and beauty. The transformation of the sea-nymph presents the myth of Daphne and Apollo. The sea-nymph Ileuthyeria also attracted Tritons. They wanted to seduce her. She saved herself through transformation into coral. The colour of coral substance shows the performance of beauty. The description as "the coral face undrew wave-tinge/Rose paleness under water shift"—presents a subtle view of natural surrounding. Nonetheless, lifeless trees convey the sense of fear. The protagonist shares the tragic process of the transformation of the sea-nymph into coral:

> The smooth brows, seen, and half seen,
> now ivory stillness.
> And So-shu churned in the sea, So-shu also,
> using the long moon for a churn-stick....
>
> (*EZRA POUND The Cantos*, p. 9)

In the above lines Pound juxtaposes two images which are drawn from Chinese and the Mediterranean sources. So-shu is turned into the reflection of the moon visible in the water of the ocean. The sea shore looks crowded with a number of characters like Poseidon, Tyro, and Proteus. The picture of evening, colour of the sand and small animals present a succession of images which are juxtaposed with each other. The Mediterranean beauty of the first canto is continued in Canto II. The long lines of the first Canto provided a correlation with strong sweeping waves of the sea. But in this Canto, as the water changes, the rhythm and music of small lines denote quick movements. The three visions which present episodes of transformational themes, convey the experiences of love, fear and greed.[33] The Canto ends with "And...." in which the epical correlations lead us to next Canto.

The third Canto begins with the protagonist of the poem who continues his journey of experience that he gains from history, culture, and living conditions of human beings. The poet presents a living history of the Western culture, which suffers from sheer wastage. The narrator faces disorder, decay and immorality. The Renaissance is reviewed in this context.

The Cantos, to some extent, are autobiographical revelations of facts. The subjective persona brings the experience of the poet's own struggle. In the beginning of the Canto, the poet presents his own suffering. After America, Pound reached England via Venice. His visit to Venice was full of hardships. He was almost penniless. While returning from Venice, on a stopover in Paris Pound was unable to purchase even a book, namely the *Iliad,* in Latin, which priced only four francs. His visit to Venice was important for many reasons. He, in June 1908, in Venice, published his first collection of poems *A Lume Spento.* He spent whatever little money he had with him.[34] The Canto opens with the description of staircase of Venice customhouse with the Mediterranean beauty of the sea.

The big ship "Buccentoro" mentioned by Pound in this poem refers to the ship Bucintoro used by Doge of Venice, is presented with its association of Venice and Adriatic. The description of waves as the Italian song "Stretti," portrays the beauty of sea surge. Kore or Persephone appears, then with her beauty: The experience of the narrator of Venice is related to the experience of Tuscan Gods. The line "Greenveins in the turquoise," refers to a big Egyptian scrarab in British Museum. It gave Pound an insight into Egyptian culture and civilization; and the latter part of the poem deals with the theme of Cid and of Ignez de Castro. Cid, known as Rodrigo Diaz de Bivar (1040-1099), was a Spanish soldier. He served under Sancho IV of Navarre. Later he also served the Arab Kings of Sargossa. He appears as the hero of the Spanish epic "Poema del Cid."[35] And Ignez de Castro was a noble woman (1320-1355). Pedro, the Prince of Portugal, after the death of his first wife, married her. But King Alfonso IV killed her because he did not trust her. When Alfonso died, Pedro took her body from the grave and put her on the throne, and the courtiers were asked to pay respect to the dead queen.[36] The Spanish and Portuguese episodes present violence and drear waste. The picture of palace at Mantua, juxtaposes the ideogrammatic facts together:

> Ignez da Castro murdered, and a wall
> Here stripped, here made to stand.

Drear waste, the pigment flakes from the stone,
Or plaster flakes, Mantegna painted the wall.
Silk tatters, 'Ned Spe Nec Metu'.

(*EZRA POUND The Cantos*, p. 12)

"Silk tatters" show no hope and no fear for future-waste and violence. The first three Cantos in the beginning form the main approach to the treatment of the rest of the Cantos. They provide an objective history which presents permanent, recurrent and casual values. The first Canto projects the world of Grecian history in Odyssean theme. The Roman history through Ovid's *The Metamorphoses* is presented in the second Canto and the third Canto deals with the Western history. The protagonist picks up a timeless history of past devastation and makes his journey adventurous and romantic. He passes through the dark territories of the human civilization and struggles to find out order. He travels through his own state of mind too.

The next four Cantos, IV-VII, present the glimpses of reality. These Cantos belong to phantastikon of Ezra Pound. The word phantastikon was used by Greek psychologists, who presented "sundry patches of the macrocosm."[37] The particular consciousness again presents the psychic experience of archetypal characters. The metamorphosis presents the moments of hard realities which give a wider significance to the totality of human experience. Canto IV portrays episodes of moral passion from Greek and Provencal mythology. The Canto begins with the description of the city, Dioce, Troy, in contrast appears with its ruins. The vision of the ideal city also appears.

The word "Aurunculeia," is an epithet drawn from Catullus which means the praise of the bride. Aurunculeia presents a paradisal vision. Cadmus then appears as a founder of Thebes. He stands as a maker of great civilization. Through these glimpses, the vision of Dionysian delight becomes meaningful in the expression "Choros nympharum." The experience of sexual savage act is presented through the Provencal myth of Cabestan and the Ovidian myth of Tereusm Procne and

Philomela. The story presents destruction and violence. The classical and Provencal characters change themselves into each other and convey the value of sexual debasement. The lines communicate the sense of pity and fear:

And she went toward the window and cast her down,
    "All the while, the while, swallows crying:
Ityn!
    "It is Cabestan's heart in the dish."
    "It is Cabestan's heart in the dish?
    "No other taste shall change this."
And she went toward the window,
                the slim white stone bar
Making a double arch;
Firm even fingers held to the firm pale stone:
Swung for a moment,
                and the wind out of Rhodez
Caught in the full of her sleeve.

                ...the swallows crying:
"Tis, 'Tis, 'Ytis"!

(*EZRA POUND The Cantos*, pp. 13-14)

The Ovidian ladies Philomela and Procne were metamorphosed as nightingale and swallow. Tereus, who raped Philomela, was served with the flesh of his son Itys. The story of Guillema da Cabestanh and his love for Soremonda, wife of Ramond of Chateau Roussillon, presents the portrayal of destruction. Cabestan was killed by his master and his heart was served to his beloved.[38] History and myth, thus, are blended together. Procne and Soremonda are changed into "she" of the first line. The last line "'Tis, 'Tis, Ytis" is a repetition of "Itys"; and the movement creates the sound of a song of Swallow in Ovid's story.

The plot of the poem develops with another theme of metamorphosis. Actaeon was transformed into a stag by Diana. The description of Diana while bathing with nymphs in the pool of Gargaphia is visual: "Shaking, air alight with the goddess/fuming their hair in the dark,/lifting, lifting and waffing:/ Ivory dipping in silver,/ Shadow'd, o'er shadow'd." The Actaeon story is interwoven with the episode of a Provencal poet Piere Vidal who dressed himself in wolf-skins to chase Loba de Perrautier. He was killed by hounds during a hunt. In concluding stanza "Ecbatan" is presented as the vision of an ideal city of Dioce, an earthly Paradise. The city refers to the ancient capital of Media Magna that was found in 6th century BC by the first king of the Medas, Deioces. The city was surrounded by several walls which consisted of beautiful coloring and the citadel.[39] The Canto ends with feminine consciousness of beauty.

Canto V presents the picture of evil, and an unnatural city; images of order also appear in its contrast. The Ecbatan theme of previous Canto, begins in the beginning of this Canto. The clock appears as order. Ecbatan conceptualises stagnation. Diana presents the eternal feminine beauty. The depiction of Egyptian civilization and its destruction is remarkably presented. The spiritual stasis indicates the moral loss of values. Egypt was attached and ruined by Cambyses. Time looks back to find out treacherous events of history. The narrator, brings a contrast against the 'crowd' 'rushing on populous business,' that destroys the city. But the images of spiritual order are drawn from the Neo-Platonic concept of beauty: "Measureless seas and stars,/ Iamblichus' light,/ the souls ascending." The last Dantean reference of "the souls ascending," points out the world of Jupiter that presents light and order.

Roman history is portrayed in its grandeur as well as decline. The adultrated love is described in the expression "Sextus had seen her." The ideogram of Sextus Propertius and Cynthia, and Aurunculeia, are juxtaposed with ideal and false love. Saphho appears in "Atthis" and communicates barrenness, infidelity and immorality. The three Troubadour characters, Poicebot, Piere Vidal and Giovanni Borgia narrate the incidents of violence and violaton of moral code of conduct. The tale of Piocebot who became a monk, narrates the story of lust and immoral love. He left his wife and went to England. His wife fell in love with a knight. She became pregnant. Later on she became a prostitute. Poicebot, when came back from London, went to prostitutes to satisfy his lust where he met his wife. He found in her "changed and familiar face."

Pieire de Maensac showed his faith in love. He was a poor knight of Auvergne. He ran away with the wife of Bernart de Tierci and took her to the castle of Robert, Dauphin of Auvergne. When de Tierci tried to regain his wife, Pieire de Maensac defeated Tierci and protected his beloved.[40] Giovanni Borgia was killed and was found in the Tiber. His brother Cesare had his hand in Borgia's murder. The persona of the poet goes through such immoral activities of love. The old civilization presents unnatural love and violence. Time presents disorder. The consciousness of the speaker of the poem bears the burden of immorality which confronts his vision of beauty found in Aphrodite and Dante's Paradise.

The next Canto of the Phantastikon group deals with the sexual urge as the natural passion. The Canto VI is written in the form of monologue. Eleanor appears in two contexts. She represents Helen who was the destroyer of city and men.

> The stone is alive in my hand, the crops
> will be thick in my death-year...
> Till Louis is wed with Eleanor
> And had (He, Guillaume) a son that had to wife
> The Duchess of Normandia whose daughter
> Was wife to King Henry e maire del rei jove...
>
> (*EZRA POUND The Cantos*, p. 21)

Eleanor was also the daughter of William X of Acquitaine. She married Louis VII of France and afterwards Henry II of England. Thus, Eleanor of Troy and Eleanor of Aquitaine are transformed into each other and the narrator presents the vision of sexual indiscrimination. Alice, wife of Eblis III, fell in love with troubadour poet Bernart de Ventadour (1148-95). He wrote songs for her "My lady of Ventadour." When Alice found

Bernart making love with his wife he banished him from his court and imprisoned his wife in a tower.[41] Sordello, an Italian troubadour fell in love with Cunizza da Romano, wife of Count Ricciardo di San Bonifazzio. Sordello was compelled to flee to Provence. He wrote an important poem, *planh* which deals with the death of Blacatz.[42] The fascination for a lady is a natural passion which is presented in Provencal episodes. Poetry is regarded as a great art. Bernart de Ventadour wrote songs for his beloved which are very important in Provencal poems.

Eleanor also appears in Canto VII. The Canto projects the mood of Mauberley. The cultural and artistic sterility of the western Europe is portrayed in a miniature form. The Canto shows the decay of beauty and loss of true love in modern times. Helen of Canto II, as allusions from Homer to Aeschylus, appears in the beginning of this Canto. Eleanor again appears as the lady of Aquitaine. Pound mentions her in the bracket "(she spoiled in a British climate)"; and she also stands as Helen of Troy. The narrator of the poem passes through Greek, Flaubert, Henry James, London, and meets women in various forms and posits a modern treatment of passion of love and beauty.

The narrator presents "rooms, against chronicles." Images such as "empty rooms," "older houses," "the old rooms" etc. present the decline of taste of the twentieth century civilization. The historical events of tawdriness deepen the sense of loss and the scene presents the most disappointing phase of a culture. The beauty of Helen follows "phantom Rome." Ovid's metamorphoses present a kind of sexual prevention. But the passion of love in Provencal poetry glorified the theme of war. The speaker of the poem demonstrates the process of decline in European poetry from the time of the Renaissance to the twentieth century Europe. The Flaubertian three-line quotation refers to a dead civilization. The autobiographical facts remind the poet's persona of his own losses. The protagonist tries to capture the vision of beauty which is destroyed by British establishment, social fashion, and the first world war. Henry James also appears as a phantom like Tiresias. The description of Pound's visit to Paris during 1920-21 points out the haunting vision of Helen who seem to be "knocking at empty rooms, seeking for buried beauty." The whole scene is an ironic presentation of trivial background:

> And the sun-tanned, gracious and well-formed fingers
> Lift no latch of bent bronze, no Empire handle
> Twists for the knocker's fall; no voice to answer.
> A Strange concierge, in place of the gouty-footed.
>
> (*EZRA POUND The Cantos*, p. 25)

Tawdry taste in poetry and missing vision of beauty are grouped together which communicate a kind of spiritual deadness. "The old men's voices" and the "old voice" appear at every interval and makes the protagonist all the time conscious of the horror of crude reality. The twentieth century poetic style is condemned as "Paper, dark brown and stretched/ Flimsy and damned partition." In contract Ezra Pound mentions his own two poems "Ione, Dead The Long Year" and a Chinese translation "Liu Ch'e" which present the vision of lasting beauty. The sarcastic tone describes the sadness of plight. The mocking persona attacks the attitude: "Bear-bottle on the statue's pediment." The hollow men are seen talking meaningless things. The complete barrenness is pointed out sarcastically:

> And all that day, another day:
> Thin husks I had known as men,
> Dry casques of departed locusts
> speaking a shell of speech...
> Propped between chairs and table...
> Words like the locust-shells, moved by no inner being;
> A dryness calling for death;
>
> (*EZRA POUND The Cantos*, p. 26)

In the above lines, images are condensed with facts. "Thin husk," "Dry casques," "departed locusts," "words like the locust-shells," "a dryness calling for death," present the portrait of the all round decline of a society. The image of "locust" also refers to the idea of barrenness in vegetation caused by swarming locusts and shells produce the sense of horrors of war.[43] There is no passion at all. The description of social values is more damaging. Images of "husk talk," "casques," and "locust" are again repeated. The presentation is artistically moving; "Bend to the tawdry table,/ Lift up their spoons to mouths put forks in cutlets,/ And make sound like the sound of voices." This portrayal belongs to a particular class which does not possess the "inner being." The spiritual order and the will is missing in the habitants. The men and women are even worse than Ebionde, a sinner in Dante's hell. Ebionde, though a sinner, possessed, at least, passion and grandeur. These four Cantos present sundry patches of reality which manifest chaotic experiences of life.

Pound treats history in the most objectified manner. Cantos VIII to XI deal with Italian history. Three Cantos belong to the Renaissance. The historical characters like Sigismundo Malatesta, Pisanello, and Plenthon Leon Battista, are brought together who become archetypes like mythical characters. They appear as men of order. Pound's history is a perceptive method of presentation of truths. He does not present history in a systematic manner. In the Cantos, moments and events occur and they throw light on particular aspect of the events. But the factive personalities are men of action as the history of culture is the history of ideas into action. The narrator in the poem presents some facts from Chinese, American and Italian history, and communicates the mode of stirring facts of experience, with juxtaposition of values of order and disorder together.

Pound finds in history a kind of contemporaneity as he has himself remarked: "All ages are contemporaneous."[44] The temporal episodes, and actions of heroes present the action of archetypes which denote a kind of the "direction of will." To some extent, these heroes and heroines in their treatment are romanticized, but they present objective reality of life. History in Cantos is synthetic and gives a number of personae who are not pieces of a museum. The concept of history in Cantos as "a category of knowledge"[45] seems to be a wrong assessment. Pound presents events and facts which form a sequence of ideas. There is always a conflict between apocalypse and beautiful vision of the protagonist of the poem. The facts and figures are ideograms. If history provides knowledge, it also presents good traditions. The narrative sequence crops up with ideas of action.

Cantos VIII-XI, are condensed images of the Renaissance. The Italian background had already appeared in several Cantos. The Italian neo-Platonism attracted Pound for its achievement of art and architecture. Sigismundo Malatesta and other characters present the history of war and political intrigue. Sigismundo Malatesta was the most famous figure among all the Malatestas who belonged to a family of war mongers. They belonged to the area of Rimini. Sigismundo Malatesta was the son of Malatesta Pandolfo. Malatesta Robert was the son of Sigismundo Malatesta. Sigismundo built the Tempio Malatestiano in Rimni. He fought against the Catholicism of Pope Pius II. He had an active political career. He also fought against his own brother. He fell in love with Isotta, daughter of Fransesa di Atto. But he married two ladies one after another. He was a great soldier. But Pound is interested in him for his love for art and his true love for Isotta. He also stands as a "true representative of the Renaissance."[46]

Sigismundo was a great humanist. He gave due honour to artists who painted the Chapel frescoes of the Tempio. It was a great monument. The temple shows Sigismundo's love for pagan beauty. His fight against Papal authorities exposes a strong sense of protest against the rotten values of religion. The paganism, which is reflected in the design of roof, statues, and pillars of the temple is opposed by the fourteenth century Christian values. In Italian religious concept, Ezra Pound finds a kind of disorder and treats the contemporary repressive attitude a destructive force which is responsible for the decline of civilization.

The beginning of Canto VIII seems to be the parody of T.S. Eliot's line "These fragments I have shored against my ruins." Pound parodies it: "These fragments you have shelved (shored)." The persona of the poem refers to his effort of finding out past values. The remarks "slut," and "Bitch" present the anger of the protagonist. Three Italian characters, Alessandro,

Giohanni, and Giznozio figure in the Canto. Alessandro, the Duke of Florence, was killed by his kinsman Lorenzino de Medici. Giohanni was a Florentine merchant. Gianozio was a chancellor to Sigismundo. The place is Florence which stands for beauty, art and political activities of the fourteenth century Italy. The description refers to a correspondence between Sigismundo Malatesta and Giohanni. Sigismundo wrote letters from the battlefield. The letter mentions the details about painters who were hired by Sigismundo Malatesta. Sigismundo promises to make them due payment for their art. Pound makes his hero a humanist, because generally artists suffer from exploitation. The usura makes artist ill-paid. In his letter Sigismundo mentions his activities as a stout soldier:

> Venice has taken me on again
> At 7,000 a month, *fiorini di Camera.*
> For 2,000 horse and four hundred footmen,
> And it rains here by the gallon,
> We have had to dig a new ditch.
> In three or four days
> I shall try to set up the bombards.
>
> (*EZRA POUND The Cantos,* p. 30)

The letter ends with the description of Sigismundo's activities and the Canto ends with "and..." which extends its narrative technique to the next Canto. It again denotes the epical framework.

Canto IX deals with war, and presents the facts of death of many warriors. The beginning of the Canto deals with the hardships and natural calamities. The description of the Tempio and its art is remarkable:

> First: Ten slabs best red, seven by 15, by one third,
> Eight ditto, good red, 15 by three by one,
> Six of same, 15 by one by one.
> Eight columns 15 by three and one third
> etc... with carriage, danars 151.
>
> (*EZRA POUND The Cantos,* p. 38)

The details of construction material show the art of minute description. The marvelous pagan beauty is projected through elephants, the Zodiac, Diana and symmetrical linings of the walls of Chapels. The narrator of the Canto conveys the sense of beauty. Marble reached to Rimni by water and land. The beautiful carvings of the temple conveyed the "feeling," "breathing," and "tranquil vivid astonishment of stones."[47] The protagonist of the poem discards the repressive attitude of Christian power embodied in Pope Pius II and Aeneas silvius Piccolomini. Sigismundo calls "little runt Andreas," and Pius II is described as a "monstrous swollen, swelling s.o.b." These religious men were cruel and callous. The next Canto again presents the details of Sigismundo's soldiership.

These Cantos are poems of major *Personae*. Pound presents Sigismundo as a man of great action. The narrator presents the sensibility of the character who faces a hostile situation in his time. These three Cantos (Malatesta Cantos) present several facts of political, economic and artistic conditions of the fourteenth century Italy. The facts are taken from quotations and pronouncements. The narrator himself puts on a mask of Sigismundo and presents a historical record of achievement of Malatesta's art. Sigismundo Malatesta is an objectified persona who, sometimes, also expresses the point of view of the poet.

In his quest the protagonist descends into hell, which is the contemporary history of Europe. The quest theme began in the opening of the first Canto with its Odyssean scaffold. But in the hell Cantos (XIV-XV), Pound uses Dante's Inferno not as a geographical location but as a presentation of ideas of consciousness. About these Cantos, Pound, in one of his letters says that "the hell cantos are specifically London, the state of English mind in 1919 and 1920."[48] The poet in these Cantos presents usurers, profiteers and abusers of language. At great length, Pound discusses Inferno and shows his main interest in Dante and his values, and he finds his own hell that "reeks with money."[49] Usura is the greatest evil. The lower circle of Inferno of Dante is also full of cheats and usurers. These hell cantos appear in contrast with the moral theme of Cantos XII and XIII, in which Confucian values are presented.

Canto XIII is the first Confucian Canto. In this Canto, quotations from Chinese sources establish the code of moral values. They are taken from Ta Hio and Chung-Yung. Kung in this poem presents wisdom and a sense of order. He stands as a nation builder. In the previous Canto, Sigismundo stood as a temple-builder. The narrator, in his conversational mode, talks about the sense of order which is concerned with subjects like defence, province, ritual temple, and art of observation. The entire Canto is written in the colloquial tone. The narrator emphasizes the need of an external order and character. The last three lines are ironical in their affirmation:

> The blossoms of the apricot
> blow from the east to the west,
> And I have tried to keep them from falling.
>
> (*EZRA POUND The Cantos*, p. 60)

The protagonist loses his hold over order in Canto XIV which begins with his hell experience. The opening line *"Io venni in luogo d'ogni luce muto"* refers to Dante's Inferno which presents the hell proper. The location of the hell starts with circle one which is without light; and it is crowded with sinners. The first few lines present them with fearful gestures:

> Faces smeared on their rumps,
> wide eye on flat buttock,
> Bush handing for heart,
> Addressing crowds through their arse-holes,
>
> (*EZRA POUND The Cantos*, p. 61)

In the above lines Pound presents portraits of politicians. profiteers, financiers, publishers; and betrayers of language also appear with their vices who meet condemnation and contempt. The Canto presents perverts of all kind. The present world is worse than hell:

> the blowing of dry dust and stray paper,
> foetor, sweat, the stench of stale oranges,
> dung, last cess-pool of the universe,
> mysterium, acid of sulphur,
> the pusillanimous, raging;

plunging jewels in mud,
            and howling to find them unstained;
sadic mothers driving their daughters to bed with decreptidue,
sows eating their litters.

(*EZRA POUND The Cantos*, p. 62)

Usura finds its deceptive and malicious role in spoiling the human relationship between mothers and daughters. The "sadic mothers," because of unavoidable circumstances, compel their daughters to become victims of lust and passion; this is a pathetic narration of great social evil. The deep hell is full of nasty and nauseating experience. The sinners are presented ugly and frightful. In their changing shape they look "melting like dirty wax." These sinners are murderers and spiritual perverts. Calvin, the French Protestant theologian, is one of them who justified interest on money. St. Clement of Rome allowed property and wealth to be possessed even by religious men. The protagonist expresses his hatred contemptuously:

            Above the hell-rot
the great arse-hole
            broken with piles,
hanging stalactites,
            greasy as sky over Westminister.

(*EZRA POUND The Cantos*, p. 62)

Images of "arse-hole," "broken with piles," and "greasy as sky over Westminster" present a scatological portrait of a sinister world; satire, finally ends in obscenity. The liars are presented as "the soil living pus, full of vermin." In the concluding lines of the Canto the narrator meets non-serious scholars of the 1920s. They were real "obstructors of knowledge" and "obstructors of distribution" of good literature. These sinners are without dignity. But they have caused great harm to literary world of Pound's London.

Canto XV is like Dantean Inferno. It is confessional in tone. The narrator presents a landscape in which trees present the state of mind. The Canto also presents a passing vision of purgatory in which great poets appear and they resent against the working of evil. The kingdom of Dis presents the vision of horror of the war and the Russian Revolution. The sardonic tone is satirical in its attack on contemporary writers:

> In this bolge bores are gathered,
> Infinite pus flakes, scabs of a lasting pox.
>
> (*EZRA POUND The Cantos*, p. 65)

Hatred leads us to climax. The second line is Dantesque. The protagonist tries to wipe off the effect of sin by bathing "in alkali and in acid." The speaker in the Canto makes his descent into hell: "blind with the sun light,/ swollen-eyed, rested,/ lids sinking, darkness unconscious." Canto XVI deals with the destruction caused by the First World War. The poet is the guide in this hell. He passes through the hell of rich men, and enters into the world of lovers and founders of cities. The description of hell presents river, trees, bush, road, and the two mountains—one is Purgatorio, and the second is a steel mountain. In the hell, Peire Cardinal and other criminals are brought together.

The protagonist tries to sleep on the grass, and in his sleeplessness he hears voices, which narrate great events of past. Franz Joseph, Emperor of Austria, is seen with troops, trenches, and machine guns. In war even children were killed; and after their death, they are seen howling and crying for their mothers. The protagonist hears the Russian revolutionaries advancing and marching. The scene presents a picture of ruthless massacre. A smiling boy was killed at Moscow station. The Canto ends with the cruel strategies of war-mongers. The three Cantos, in short, present a real hell that was Europe during 1920s.

T.S. Eliot criticized Pound's hell from his Anglican point of view. He described it as a comfortable hell, because it fails to distinguish a necessary evil from the great social sin. The main complaint of T.S. Eliot is that measures, like Dante's sinners, don't have magnanimity in their suffering; and the whole hell seems to be less effective and least convincing.[51]

Pound's major concern with evil is usura. He presents a kind of political, moral and aesthetic disorder. Usura as the main source of human suffering belongs to the medieval world. The interest on money was justified by the Church and Greek philosophers. Plato (Laws, V, 742) and Aristotle (Politics, I, XXI) treat it as a part of nature. But money-lending begins exploitation. Pound is only concerned with the reality of evil as it has existed in all ages. He dislikes the idea of glorifying it as presented in Satan of *Paradise Lost.* In one of his letters Pound condemns Protestantism which "has lost the sense of mental and spiritual *rottenness.* Dante has it: "gran sacco chef a merda."[52] Pound presents the mental and spiritual rottenness in his hell Cantos.

Pound presents a world of apocalypse. The hell, in this context, presents waste, ruins, chaos and suffering. He depicts a demonic society as "existential hell," like Dante's *Inferno,* or the hell that man creates on earth, as in *1984, No Exist,* and *Darkness at Noon.*[53] In a demonic real world, like Pound's hell, love betrays its genuine feeling. Images of "weapons," armour" and "dead mechanism" present unnatural and inhuman world. This demonic world in modern literature points out the low mimetic structure of experience, and the conflict is always between trivial society and the concept of romantic idealization of life. Pound's first thirty Cantos, in the light of Frye's analysis of demonic society as apocalypse, present demonic images of real hell. The poem presents a vision of evil as an existential evil. The images as "smeared faces," "the soil, living pus," "dead maggots," "usurers sitting on piles of stone books," "slum flesh," "infinite pus flakes," "steel mountain," "blue lakes of acid," "fallen louse eggs," "water reeds," "machine gun," and "troops" present the demonic world of perversion, and apocalypse which threaten the social stability and existence of natural order.

From Canto XVII to Canto XXVII, we have Italian background and a historical experience of disorder. The narrator from modern world, goes back to history and tries to enrich his knowledge with more experience. Cantos XVIII and XIX deal with war and sabotage. In Canto XIX the voice of Cosimo de Medici is heard and the narrator of the poem speaks, because he witnesses the ruins of Italy. The poet presents three visions of Venice. Venice is projected through water, its beautiful mountains, with its gods, and subterranean glimpses of its natural beauty.

The next three Cantos (XXIV, XXV and XXVI) deal with Venice with its decay and achievements. These poems are the Cantos of Venice. In Pound's poetry cities present several phases of civilization. In later Cantos Wagadu and Byzantium appear as the centres of great civilization. These three Cantos deal with maturity, death and decline of Venice. The Canto XXIV investigates historical facts of Venetian decay The protagonist describes the activities of medieval and Renaissance heroes who throw light on the grandeur of the history of Venice. Niccolo d'Este, a ruler of Ferrara travels to many places. He feels pleasure with his Greek experience which is contrasted with the commercialization of holy places. The epitaph mentions the irony:

> 'Albert made me, Tura painted my wall,
> And Julia the Countess sold to a tannery....
>
> (*EZRA POUND The Cantos*, p. 114)

Alberto d'Este, father of Niccolo d'Este, built the palace and Tura painted the walls of Ferrara, which is "paradise dei Sarti." But Julia the Countess who owned the Schifanoja, used it as a tobacco factory.[54] Ferrara presents the process of an eternal degeneration. Canto XXV presents the failure of the city. Venice, at first moves with Eleusinian tradition and presents the beauty of Aphrodite. But it posits itself, in the end, as a heap of dead stones. The Venice with its past grandeur passes through the description of kings, queens, and palaces, architectonic design of pillars, staircases, arches and river. The presentation is ideogrammic:

> Which is to say: they built out over the arches
> and the palace hangs there in the dawn, the mist,
> in that dimness,
> or as one rows in from past the murazzi
> the barge slow after moon-rise
> and the voice sounding under the sail.
>
> (*EZRA POUND The Cantos*, p. 117)

Canto XXVI deals with Italian history. But the tone of the narrator is elegiac. Venice is presented through facts and documents.

The protagonist, despite his experience, finds an antithesis to disorder. In Canto XX he establishes the concept of paradise. The poet presents experience of his visit to Italy, France and Germany: "And that year I went up to Freiburg." The picture of a beautiful world is presented. The protagonist expresses his delightful experience as he lived in these places:

> Between the two lower meadows; sound,
> The sound, as I have said, a nightingale
> Too far off to be heard.
> And the light falls, *remir*,
> from her breast to thighs.
>
> (*EZRA POUND The Cantos*, p. 90)

This Canto presents the ideograms of action. History, passion and persons present the beauty of Venice in glimpses.

But the last Canto of *A Draft of XXX Cantos* ends with evil. It is almost a lyrical poem. The narrator deals with pity as evil and sentimentality of modern civilization. The Canto's first line echoes Artemis' lovely song. The concept of evil equates time because the protagonist loses the facts of order as he goes through recurrent aspects of history. Artemis stands for permanent truth which inspired the narrator not to get disappointed with casual realities of life. Artemis is the goddess of wild life and the hunt. The Canto begins:

> Compleynt, compleynt I hearde upon a day,
> Artemis singing, Artemis, Artemis
> Agaynst Pity lifted her wail:
> Pity causeth the forests to fail,
> Pity slayeth my nymphs,
> Pity spareth so many an evil thing.
> Pity befouleth April,
> Pity is the root and the spring.
>
> (*EZRA POUND The Cantos*, p. 147)

The opening description presents a pastiche of medieval sources. It narrates the story of murder of Ignez' da Castro and Madam Hyle. Pity is the counterpart of usura, the cause of all evils. The evil elaborated in this canto does not indicate organic time. Pity is a fraudulent emotion which exploits everything. The narrator explains the horror of evil through episodes.

Paphos presents the suppression of youthful desire. Castro was a noble woman whom Pedro secretly married. But king Alfonso IV killed her. Pedro, her husband, exhumed her body and placed on a throne at his side to pay homage to the dead queen.[55] Pity is seen as a violence of natural order. Evil is presented through archetypal characters like Artemis and historical figures like Pedro, and Ignez da Castro. The narrator faces a conflict between the Grecian vision of the world and the Christian world of today. The Canto ends with "Il Papa mori," which refers to Pope Alexander VI who died in 1503. The end of the poem indirectly points out of the end of the western tragedy which is the theme of the XXX Cantos. The first part of the Canto is lyrical. It is like an elegy.

A Draft of XXX Cantos is a modern epic written in encyclopaedic form. The poet deals with a kaleidoscopic vision and experience. The poem narrates a history, and the ideas are presented in a discountinous form. Negative and positive images of culture are put in contrast because of the largeness of the poetic plot. The poem contains juxtaposed images, which condense the expression of facts and direct addresses provide colloquial diction and objectivity. They attack and criticize the prevailing situation. In this poem, characters, episodes, factual details, etc. appear from history which provide instances for metaphorical expression and a structure based on the theory of similitude and contrast, as it is in *The Waste Land.*[56]

The Cantos appear as a poem of civilization. The poem as a whole presents a cycle of vast experience which combines objective, subjective, mythical and historical images of experience. Therefore, being a poem of experience, its content is realistic or low mimetic.[57] The Cantos are a kind of cultural criticism. The protagonist gather several sorts of experience, which expose many themes. The quest is made in two forms—the Odyssean and the Dantean. These adhere to three patterns of experience—permanent, recurrent, and casual. The experiences gathered by the poet and the protagonist are experiences of Inferno, Purgatory, and Paradise. Pound had a clear division of things in his mind. The enclosure below this page shows his scheme for XXX Cantos. Pound's jottings show his treatment of subjects through Greek, Italian, and modern history. Hell, Purgatory and Paradise define and assess various subjects. The summary of the XXX Cantos as given in his scribblings, give us an idea of his plan.[58]

A Schema for XXX Cantos

On the back of an undatable form on which the management of the Hotel Excelsor, Frankfurt a, M., solicited the comments of guests, Pound penciled a scheme for the first 30 Cantos, which (subject to errors in my decipherment of his scribble) ran as follows:

nek–
metam–
< cid
rep–
inchoate
murder
Eleanor
=
Sidg.

Baldy
Kung.
Hell
Purg
War

Par. Ter.
fraud
20 Par. Este-sacrif.

21 Medici Gib
Este I, II, III
25-6 Venice
27 Bolshoi

space (Travell)
Pernella
Cunizza
mind - (metaphys)

Pity

"Nek-" and "metam" are in Greek characters. "Rep-" is presumably repeat." I wish I felt sure of "inchoate;" it looks more like "incubate." The horizontal line after "War" marks the division between I-XVI and XVII-XXVII as originally published. "Par" would be "Paradise," unless it's "Parisina," whom Nic Este had beheaded ("sacrif'). "Gib" is Gibraltar. At the top right we have a summary of XXVIII-XXX, which were added after XVII-XXVII were published in 1928, to make the total XXX Cantos. "Space" and "Travell[ers]" pertains to 28, Pernella, Cunizza and "mind—(metaphys)" to 29, "Pity" of course to 30. Since there was room for the notes on these three cantos at the bottom of the sheet, his placing it where he did may possibly mean something.

NOTES & REFERENCES

1. *Dial*, LXXIX (December 1925), pp. 501-02.
2. Eda Lou Walton, "Obscurity in Modern Poetry," *New York Times Book Review*, V (2 April 1933), p. 2.
3. Geoffery Grigson, "The Methodism of Ezra Pound," *New Verse*, 5 (October 1933), pp. 20-21.
4. Consider, for example, George Dekker, *Sailing After Knowledge: The Cantos of Ezra Pound, A Critical Appraisal* (London: Routledge, 1963), p. 107: "Cantos are not a poem but a conspiracy"; Forest Read, "A Man of Fortune," *Motive and Method in the Cantos of Ezra Pound*, ed. Lewis Leary (New York: Columbia University Press, 1954), p. 101: "The Cantos appear to be formless because of Pound's apparently unfathomable literary and historical allusions. Moreover complaints are that sections of the Cantos are dull and verbose"; Noel Stock, *Reading the Cantos: A Study of Meaning in Ezra Pound* (London: Routledge & Kegan Paul, 1965), p. 10: "There is no principle of unity in these (XXX) Cantos, atleast twenty of which suffer from major obscurities. The most we can say is that they bear every sign of Pound's authorship. This is the one unity visible at present"; Richard Peever, "Notes on the Cantos of Ezra Pound," *Hudson Review*, XXV, 1, Spring, 1972, p. 51: "There is a feeling of wholeness in the Cantos that is very hard to explain. It may be, in part, that Pound's work represents a wide range of modulations of a single voice. But it is worse than that."
5. Hugh Kenner, *The Poetry of Ezra Pound* (London: Faber and Faber, 1950), pp. 280-81.
6. Daniel D. Pearlmen, *The Barb of Time: On the Unity of Ezra Pound's Cantos* (New York: Oxford University Press, 1969), pp. 26-27.
7. *Literary Essays of Ezra Pound*, ed. T.S. Eliot (London: Faber and Faber, 1968), p. 394.
8. *Ibid.* p. 86.
9. *Ibid.*, p. 9.
10. *The Selected Letters of Ezra Pound*, ed. D.D. Paige (London: Faber and Faber, 1971), p. 210.

11. Y.B. Yeats, "A Packet for Ezra Pound," *Ezra Pound: A Critical Anthology*, ed. J.P. Sullivan (Harmondsworth: Penguin Books Ltd., 1970), p. 100.
12. Walter Sutton, *American Free Verse: The Modern Revolution in Poetry* (New York: New Direction, 1973), pp. 84-85.
13. *The Selected Letters of Ezra Pound*, p. 239.
14. Ezra Pound, *The Spirit of Romance* (London: Peter Owen, 1970), p. 128.
15. Ezra Pound, *Selected Prose 1909-65*. ed. William Cookson (London: Faber and Faber, 1973), p. 30.
16. Walter Sutton, *American Free Verse*, p. 71.
17. Hugh Kenner, *The Pound Era* (London: Faber and Faber, 1972, pp. 416-17.
18. Hugh Kenner, "The Rose in the Steel Dust," *Hudson Review*, III (1950), pp. 100-01.
19. T.S. Eliot, "Isolated Superiority," *Dial*, 84 (January to June 1928), p. 6.
20. M.L. Rosenthal, "Dynamics of Form and Motive in Some Representative Twentieth-Century Lyric Poems," *ELH*, 37, I (March, 1970), p. 147.
21. Northrop Frye, *Anatomy of Criticism* (Princeton: Princeton University Press, 1973), p. 57.
22. *Ibid.*, p. 61.
23. Donald Davie, *Ezra Pound: Poet As Sculptor* (New York: Oxford University Press, 1964), p. 32.
24. Northrop Frye, *Anatomy of Criticism*, p. 318.
25. *Literary Essays of Ezra Pound*, p. 264.
26. Ezra Pound, *A Draft of XXX Cantos* (London: Faber and Faber, 1930), p. 7, Hereafter all references will be made to this source in the body of the text.
27. Hugh Kenner, *The Pound Era*, p. 149.
28. Robert Langbaum, *The Poetry of Experience* (London: Chatto and Windus, 1957), p. 94.
29. Christine Brook-Rose, *A ZBC of Ezra Pound* (London: Faber and Faber, 1957), p. 137.
30. *Ibid.*, pp. 41-42.
31. Daniel D. Pearlman, *The Barb of Time: On the Unity of Ezra Pound's Cantos*, pp. 48-49.

32. Lillian Feder, *Ancient Myth in Modern Poetry* (Princeton: Princeton University Press, 1971), p. 109.
33. Daniel D. Pearlman, *The Barb of Time*, p. 49.
34. Charles Norman, *Ezra Pound* (London: Macdonald, 1960), p. 26.
35. John Hamilton Edwards and William W. Vasse, *Annotated Index to the Cantos of Ezra Pound* (Berkeley: University of California Press, 1971), p. 51.
36. *Ibid.*, p. 32.
37. Ezra Pound, *The Spirit of Romance*, p. 92.
38. John Hamilton Edwards and William W. Vasse, *Annotated Index to the Cantos of Ezra Pound*, p. 28.
39. *Ibid.*, p. 56.
40. *Ibid.*, p. 134.
41. *Ibid.*, p. 237.
42. *Ibid.*, p. 202.
43. Daniel Pearlman, *The Barb of Time*, pp. 88-89.
44. Ezra Pound, *The Spirit of Romance*, p. 8.
45. Marius Bewley, *Mask and Mirrors* (London: Chatto and Windus, 1970), p. 303.
46. Christine Brooke-Rose, *A ZBC of Ezra Pound* (London: Faber and Faber, 1971), pp. 172-73.
47. Hugh Kenner, *The Pound Era*, p. 252.
48. *The Selected Letters of Ezra Pound*, p. 239.
49. *Literary Essays of Ezra Pound*, p. 211.
50. T.S. Eliot, "After Strange Gods: A Primer of Modern Heresy," *Ezra Pound: A Critical Anthology*, ed. J.P. Sullivan (Harmondsworth: Penguin Books Ltd., 1970), p. 184.
51. *The Selected Letters of Ezra Pound*, p. 293.
52. Northrop Frye, *Anatomy of Criticism*, pp. 147-54.
53. John Hamilton Edwards and William W. Vasse, *Annotated Index to the Cantos of Ezra Pound*, p. 106.
54. *Ibid.*, p. 32.
55. David Lodge, *The Modes of Modern Writing* (London: Edward Arnold, 1977), p. 103.
56. Northrop Frye, *Anatomy of Criticism*, p. 320.
57. Hugh Kenner, "A Schema for XXX Cantos," *Paideuma*, 2 (Fall, 1973), p. 203.

7
Conclusion

The preceding chapters have examined Ezra Pound's poetic craftsmanship, his involvement with European cultural background, and his awareness of contemporary history, of the existing social and human conditions. The examination has demonstrated that his verse is both powerful and effective, characterized by his sense of discovery of newness. As a conscious literary artist, Pound wrote verse with a clear conception of poetry and what, as a poet, he should do? His critical theories were, by their genesis, a by-product of his creative activity. In other words, they were a part and parcel of his poetic programme. His poetry and his criticism elucidate each other.

As a poet of extraordinary stature, he has, throughout his poetic career, given evidence of coherence and consistency in regard to literary principles. His integrity as a serious artist can be seen in his involvement with developing technical accomplishment. Yet, as the earlier chapters of the present study demonstrate, he had to struggle against inadequate language till 1912, and his formulation of critical theories from 1912-1920, theories that would work, have marked a visible change in the syntax and diction of his poetry. Pound also went on experimenting poetic forms between 1912 to 1916 and was, in the best sense of the term, a poet-critic and a critic-poet. That is why his criticism and poetry elucidate each other.

His vast knowledge of the literary traditions of the past, his preoccupation with the use of language in poetry, and his effort at getting a paideuma for poets—these have educated him in his career as well as other poets such as T.S. Eliot. From the beginning of his poetic career, he upheld poetry to be a great art which demanded of the practitioner careful operation, arduous discipline, and a rigorous training.

He compared poetry with science, chemistry, and medical sciences in which diagnosis is made and things are cured. A poet, too, needs to make a diagnosis of evil in literature and rediscover the cult of beauty. An artist, Pound's principles demand, should make efforts to distinguish between good and bad and avoid falsification of human facts. Pound always condemned the artificial role of the poet. The critical knowledge, as an essential part of poetry writing, is related to the knowledge of languages and cultures of other ages. By educating himself, in this way, a poet finds his own ideograph of the best traditions. The process involves comparison and selection.

Tradition, awareness, and preparation are essential for good writing. In association with the past, the poet finds the examples of maximum excellence. As an exemplification of this principle, we can see Pound's preoccupation with Dante, Villon, Arnaut Daniel, Cavalcanti, Homer, Gautier, Henry James, Flaubert and some other French writers. He acquires a knowledge of the Provencal, Chinese and Western culture. The preparation for good writing, according to Pound, also needs discrimination in order to avoid repetition. He insists on contribution and addition by new experiments.

Pound's own poetry and the writings of those under the orbit of his influence are good in this sense. Most of Pound's early poems (*Personae, Exultations*, and *Ripostes*) turn their back on the existing jejune verse and boldly experiment with new idioms, new modes of language, and new themes. To renew the language of the tribe, he undertakes translations, and bring to bear upon these his contemporary sensibility. Pound's new poetry has had to fight its way till it can be enjoyed by the taste it creates. In the Anglo-American world he stands a towering giant as the maker of modern poetry. He promoted good modern poetry by young poets and had it published in *Poetry, Glebe* and *Blast.* T.S. Eliot, James Joyce, Aldington, H.D., Flint, Ford Madox Hueffer, William Carolos Williams, and Wyndham

Lewis—to name the now most well-known ones—published their early works with Pound's efforts. His instructions to contemporary writers and poets in his letters are an evidence of his role as an architect of modern poetry in English. In one of his letters (D.D. Paige, p. 237) Pound wrote: "of course there are several things I have been trying to teach you for the past 20 years. I don't lay as much stock by teaching the elder generation as by teachin' the risin', and if one gang dies without learnin' there is always the next. Keep on remindin 'em that we ain't bolcheviks, but only the terrigyin' voice of civilization, kulchuh, refinement, aesthetic perception." Pound's correction of Eliot's poems is well-known; he even corrected a few poems of W.B. Yeats. And Yeats, though he was angry at the young Pound's impudence, changed the language of his poetry after the incident.

Pound's role in the first modernist movement in the twentieth century poetry is seen in his involvement with Imagism, Vorticism, Chinese ideogram, and the poetic theory of equations and dispersonalization of personal emotion. Imagism, under Pound's leadership, was a kind of discipline which enabled contemporary poets to purge themselves of poetic impurities. It also helped to achieve precision, exactness, compactness, hardness, scientific accuracy and objectivity. Vorticism, originally a movement in painting, was for Pound a kind of "kinetic imagism" in poetry. It yielded the technique of superimposition of images. From the Chinese ideogram Pound learnt the technique of juxtaposition which proved useful in his *Cantos*.

Some of the principles of *New Criticism* owe to Pound's conception of Imagism, Vorticism, and ideogram. T.S. Eliot's theory of the "*objective correlative*" owes to Pound, who remarks in *The Spirit of Romance*: "Poetry is a sort of inspired mathematics, which gives us equations, not for abstract figures, triangles, spheres, and the like, but equations for the human emotions." (p. 14)

In Pound's early poetry, some of the poems in *Personae* (1909) and *Exultations* (1909) achieves objectivity through the use of mask and personae. Several poems of *Ripostes* (1912) excel in the construction of vivid images and have maturity, sophistication and precision. Economy of words in these poems displays a maximum of meaning. *Hugh Selwyn Mauberley* (1920) employes juxtaposed images and multiple personae.

Pound's theories as they affect the language of poetry, concern three correlations of emotion: sound effects imagery, and diction; or, what he calls, melopoeia, phanopoeia, and logopoeia. Pound's melopoeia, among other things, encourages the use of free verse, and rejects the metronomic patterns of verse. Composing verse in terms of musical phrases brings its rhythm somewhat close to the rhythm of ordinary speech. Phanopoeia concerns visual images which help the poet to communicate precise feelings. The phanopoeia of Pound's poetry is a matter of exact, precise, and visual images. The logopoeia of Pound's poetry concerns his use of suggestive and connotative words. Pound's diction, unlike his rhythm, sometime moves away from the language of ordinary speech. His logopoeia is heavily loaded with out-of-the-way words from many foreign languages. Sometimes this affects Pound's imagery, too. In any case, it affects the otherwise very transparent language of Pound's poetry. From the point of view of the reader, this makes for rhetorical discontinuity, too. His logopoeia, however, reverberates with meaning.

The total body of Pound's poetry can be divided into the lyrical and the satirical categories. His satirical poems are lit up by his social concerns and tend to be encyclopaedic. These give us a sense of contemporary history. *Mauberley* and the *Cantos* belong here. Many of the Cantos of Pound read like miniature-epics. The satirical Cantos evoke varied responses. They are not liked by those who are admirers of modern civilization. His lyrical poems have been better appreciated than his satirical ones because they deal with beauty and love.

Pound has translated several hundred poems from Greek, Chinese, Japanese, German, Italian and Provencal. His translations act in three ways—as a window to remote culture, as criticism of social conditions, and as a glimpse into the

Poundian personae. Pound's early translations are characterized by masks, historic past, and technical accomplishments. In some poems Pound establishes a relationship with the poet of the original, in others he uses his own voice. They are marked by sincere expression and objective reality. In his longer poems (*Homage to Sextus Propertius*, *Mauberley* and *Cantos*) the best qualities of his earlier poetry are merged into something rich and complex. The negative judgement of critics on Pound's *Cantos* is due to the fact that these poems are very difficult in their allusive texture and diction and a satisfactory analysis of these poems has not yet been done. So instead of the critic judging the poetry of Pound, it is Pound's poetry that judges the limitations of the critic.

Use of allusions, quotations, and references in Pound's poetry reverberate with the cultural heritage of the past, a heritage which the modern reader has lost. As a result Pound's poetry seems difficult and obscure. In addition to this, theme is the complexity of structure in Pound's poetry. In the context of the difficulties involved, my attempt in the preceding chapters had been to elucidate difficulties. His use of historical stances, mythical and archetypal characters, and metamorphic episodes are a means of objectivity in the expression of emotion. In an age of confusion. Pound has attempted to impose an order on reality by way of images from diverse cultures. Pound's sensibility and mind tries to apprehend the crisis of our age and communicates the complex life today. He does it in a complex way, too. Pound's poetry carries the influence of Greek, Italian, Chinese, Provencal, and French literature and, in turn, has exerted great influence in the development of modern poetry.

Pound's creative translations, his use of personae, his constant preoccupation with the search for adequate language, his technical innovations and poetic craftsmanship, his mythical mode, and his involvement with literary movements with a poetic programme—these prove that Pound is among the greatest poets of the twentieth century Europe. He is the "Poets' Poet", in a real sense, and has revitalized modern poetry. As a critic, too, he has proved to be influential.

Chronology
(Life and Works: Main Events)

1885	Ezra Pound born at Haily, Idaho, 30th October, son of Homer Loomis Pound and Isabel Weston Pound. Family moves to Pennsylvania 18 months later.
1887-1901	Childhood in Wyncote, suburb of Philadelphia. Schools: Cheltenham Military Academy and Cheltenham High School.
1898	Travels to Europe with great-aunt, Gibraltar, Tunis, Venice.
1901	Travels to London with father.
1903-05	Studies at Hamilton College, Clinton, New York, Ph.B., 1905.
1906	M.A. University of Pennsylvania, Fellow in Romanics.
1906-07	Travels and studies in Spain, Provence, Italy.
1907	Instructor in Romance Languages at Wabash College, Crawfordsville, Indiana, resignation requested after four months for 'bohemian' behaviour.
1907-08	Travels in Italy.
1908	*A Lume Spento* (Venice).
	Autumn, settles in London.
	A Quinzaine for this Yule (London).
1909	*Personae, Exultations* (both London). Meets Yeats. Friendship with Ford Madox Hueffer (Ford Madox Ford). Lectures at London Polytechnic on Romance Literature.
1910	*The Spirit of Romance* (London). *Provença* (London). Works on Cavalcanti (the essay published in 1934 is dated 1910-31).
1911	*Canzoni* (London).
1912	*The Sonnets and Ballate of Guido Cavalcanti* (London). *Ripostes* (London). Writes *Patria Mia* (pub. 1950). Literary association with H.D., Richard Aldington, Wyndham Lewis, James Joyce, Yeats and others. 'Imagiste Manifesto'. Writes for 'The New Freewoman', later called 'The Egoist', and for 'The Little

	Review'. Foreign editor of 'Poetry: A Magazine of Verse' (Chicago).
1913-14	Works on Fenollosa papers. Important criticism: *Robert Frost* (Freewoman 1913, Poerry 1914), *A Few Don'ts* (Poetry 1913), *The Serious Artist* (Egoist 1913), *Troubadours, their Sorts and Conditions* (Qu. Rev. 1913), *The Later Yeats* (Poetry 1913), *Dubliners and Mr. James Joyce* (Egoist 1914), *The Renaissance* (Poetry 1914), *The Prose Tradition in Verse* (Poetry 1914), all reprinted in "The Literary Essays', 1954.
1914	Marries Dorothy Shakespear. Edits anthology *Des Imagistes.* Meets T.S. Eliot, 24th Sept. Chief contributor to 'Blast', 1914-15.
1915	*Cathay* (London). Edits *Catholic Anthology.* Preface to Poetical Works of *Lionel Johnson* [reprinted in 'Lit. Essays' 1954].
1916	*Lustra* (London). *Gaudier-Brzeska: A Memoir* (London, New York). *Certain Noble Plays of Japan,* sel. Pound, introd. Yeats (Ireland). *'Noh' or Accomplishment,* Fenollosa and Pound (London).
1917	First three *Cantos* published in 'Poetry', later withdrawn. Works on *Propertius* (pub. 1919, date given as 1917). *Dialogues of Fonteselle,* tranl. Pound (London). Main criticism: *Notes on Elizabethan Classicists* (Egoist 1917-18). *Irony, Laforgue and Some Satire* (Poetry 1917), *T.S. Eliot* (review of Prufrock, Poetry 1917). [All reprinted in 'Lit. Essays' 1954].
1918	*Pavannes and Divisions* (New York), including two essays on Dolmetsch & *A Retrospect.* Other criticism: *The Hard and Soft in French Poetry* (Poetry 1918), *Swinburne versus his Biographers* (Poetry 1918), *Henry James* (The Little Review 1918), *Joyce* (The Future 1918), *Early Translators of Greek* (Egoist 1918-19). [All reprinted in 'Lit. Essays' 1954].
1919	*Quia Pauper Amavi* (London, contains '*Three Cantos*' and '*Homage to Sextus Propertius*'). *The Fourth Canto* (London).
1920	*Hugh Selwyn Mauberley* (London). *Umbra* [early poems reprinted and translations Cavalcanti, Daniel] (London). *Instigations* [incl. essays on *Remy de Gourmont, Arnaut Daniel, Wyndham Lewis,* reprint of *Early Translators of Greek*] together with *The Chinese Written Character as a Medium for Poetry,* by Ernest Fenollosa, ed. Pound (New York).
1921	Moves to Paris. Essay on *Brancusi* (Little Review).
1922	*The Natural Philosophy of Love,* by Remy de Gourmont, transl. and introd. Pound. Correspondence with Eliot and 'editing of *The Waste Land.* Essay on *Ulysses* (Dial) [reprinted in 'Lit. Essays' 1954].

1923	*Indiscretions: or Une Revue de deux mondes* (Paris). *The Call of the Road,* by Edouard Estaunie, transl. Pound (New York).
1924	Settles Rapallo. *Antheil and the Treatise on Harmony* (Paris).
1925	*A Draft of XVI Cantos for the Beginning of a Poem of Some Length* (Paris).
1926	*Personae: Collected Poems* (New York).
1928	*A Draft of the Cantos XVII-XXVII* (London). *Ta Hio, The Great Learning* (Seattle). *Selected Poems,* introd. T.S. Eliot (London). Essays: *Dr. Williams' Position* (Dial), *How to Read* (New York Herald) [both reprinted in 'Lit. Essays' 1954].
1930	*A Draft of XXX Cantos* (Paris). *Imaginary Letters* (Paris).
1931	*How to Read* (London).
1933	*A Draft of XXX Cantos* (New York, London). *ABC of Economics* (London). Edits *Active Anthology.*
1934	*Eleven New Cantos,* XXXI-XLI (New York). *ABC of Reading* (London). *Make It New* (London) including Cavalcanti essay and *Date Line* [both reprinted in 'Lit. Essays' 1954].
1935	*Social Credit: An Impact* (London). *Alfred Venison's Poems: Social Credit Themes by the Poet of Tichfield Street* ([E.P.] (London). *Jefferson and/or Mussolini* (London).
1937	*The Fifth Decad of The Cantos* [XLII-LI] (London). *Polite Essays* (London). *Confucius, Digest of the Analects* (Milano) [later included in *Guide to Kulchur*].
1938	*Guide to Kulchur* (London; Norfolk, Conn.)
1939	Visits U.S., Honorary degree from Hamilton College. *What is Money for?* (London) [No. 3 of 'Money Pamphlets by £', ed. Russell 1951].
1940	*Cantos LII-LXXI* (London; Norfolk, Conn.). *A Selection of Poems* (London).
1940-44	Broadcasts from Rome Radio.
1941	*Italy's Policy of Social Economics 1939-40,* by Odon Por, transl. Pound (Istituto It. D'Arti Grafiche, Bergamo, Milano, Roma).
1942	*Carta da Visita di Ezra Pound* (Rome) [No. 4 of 'Money Pamphlets by £', ed. Russell].
1944.	*L'America, Roosevelt e le cause della guerra presente* (Venezia) [No. 6 of 'Money Pamphlets by £', ed. Russell]. *Oro e lavoro* (Rapallo) [No. 2 of 'Money Pamphlets by £, ed. Russell]. *Introduzione alla natura economica* degli S.U.A. (Venezia) [No. 1 of 'Money Pamphlets by £', ed. Russell].

1945	*Ciung Iung. L'asse che non vacilla* (Venezia).
	Imprisonment at Pisa (summer). Writes *Pisan Cantos.* Flown to Washington for trial on charge of treason (Nov.). Declared insane and unfit to plead, sent to St Elizabeth's Hospital for the Criminally Insane, Washington, D.C.
1947	*Confucius—The Unwobbling Pivot and The Great Digest* (Norfolk, Conn.).
1948	*The Pisan Cantos* (LXXIV-LXXXIV] (New York). *The Cantos* (I-LXXXIV) New York.
	If This be Treason (Siena).
1949	Bollingen Prize for *The Pisan Cantos.*
	Selected Poems (New York).
1954	*The Classical Anthology Defined by Confucius,* translated Pound (Cambridge, Mass.).
1955	*Section: Rock Drill, 85-95 de los cantares* (Milano).
1956	*Sophokles: Women of Trachis, a version by Ezra Pound* (London).
1958	Released from confinement, April, returns to Italy.
1959	*Thrones: 96-109 de los cantares* (Milano).
1959-60	Works on later 'Fragments', 110-116.
1962	*Love Poems of Ancient Egypt,* translated by Pound and Noel Stock from Italian version by Boris de Rachewiltz (Norfolk, Conn.).
1964	*The Cantos of Ezra Pound* (1 to 109) (London).
1969	*The Fragments* [110-117] (Norfolk, Conn.).

Bibliography

Aiken, Conrad. *Scepticisms: Notes on Contemporary Poetry*. New York: Brace and Jovanovich, Inc., 1919.

Alridge, John W. *After the Lost Generation: A Critical Study of the Writers of Two Wars*. New York: The Noonday Press, 1958.

Angolf, Charles. *The Tone of the Twenties and Other Essays*. London: Thomas Toseloff Ltd., 1966.

Alpert, Bary (ed.). *The Poet in the Imaginary Museum*. New York: Persea Books, Inc., 1978.

Baar, Ron. "Ezra Pound: Poet as Historian," *American Literature*, 42, 4 (Jan. 1971), pp. 529-30.

Banerjee, A. *Spirit Above Wars*. London: Macmillan, 1976.

Banerjee, D.K. "Dante Through the Looking Glass: Rossetti, Pound, and Eliot," *Comparative Literature*, XXIV, 2 (Spring 1972), pp. 136-42.

Baumann, Walter. *The Rose in the Steel Dust: An Examination of the Cantos of Ezra Pound*. Bern: Francke Verlag, 1967.

Ben, Kimpel D. and Eaves, C.T. "Pound's Ideogrammic Method," *American Literature*, Vol. LI, No. 2 (May 1979), pp. 205-10.

Benet, William Rose *et al.* (ed.). *The Reader's Encyclopaedia*. New York: Thomas Y. Crowell Company, 1980.

Benard, Duffey. *Poetry in America: Expression and Its Values in the Times of Bryant, Whitman and Pound*. Durham, N.C.: Duke University Press, 1978.

Bewley, Marius. *Mask and Mirror*. London: Chatto and Windus, 1970.

Blackmur, R.P. *Form and Value in Modern Poetry*. Garden City: Doubleday & Company, Inc., 1957.

Bodenheim, Maxwell. "Isolation of Carved Metal," *The Dial*, LXXII (January to June, 1922), pp. 32-33.

Bradhury, John. M. *The Fugitives: A Critical Account.* Chapel Hill: The University of North Carolina Press, 1958.

Bradhury, Malcolm and James McFarlane. *Modernism, 1890-1930.* Harmondsworth: Penguin Books, 1976.

Brett, R.L. *An Introduction to English Studies.* London: Edward Arnold Ltd., 1965.

Brooke-Rose, Christine. *A ZBC of Ezra Pound.* London: Faber and Faber, 1971.

Buchanan, Scott. *Poetry and Mathematics.* Philadelphia and New York: J.B. Lippoincott Company, 1929.

Cambon, Glauco. *The Inclusive Flame: Studies in Modern American Poetry.* Bombay: Popular Prakashan, 1969.

Carruth, Hayden. "The Poetry of Ezra Pound," *Perspectives* U.S.A., 16 (Summer 1956), p. 187.

Charles, Norman. *Ezra Pound.* London: The Macmillan Co., 1969.

Cookson, William (Ed.) *Agenda,* 4, 2 (Oct.-Nov. 1965).

——*Selected Prose, 1909-65.* London: Faber and Faber, 1973.

Cowley, Malcolm. *Exile's Return: A Literary Odyssey of the 1920's.* New York: The Viking Press, 1951.

Cowley, Malcolm (ed.). *After the Genteel Tradition: American Writers 1910-20.* Carbondale: Southern Illinois University Press, 1965.

Cown, James C. "The Classical Figures a Archytypes in Pound's Cantos I-XXX," *Twentieth Century Literature,* 6 (April 1960-Jan. 1961), pp. 25.-31.

Cunliffe, Marcus. *The Literature of the United States.* Harmondsworth: Penguin Books, 1954.

Davie, Donald. *Ezra Pound, Poet as Sculptor.* New York: Oxford University Press, 1964.

Davis, Earle. *Vision Fugitive: Ezra Pound and Economics.* Lawrence Kansas: University of Kansas Press, 1969.

Dekkar, George. *Sailing After Knowledge: The Cantos of Ezra Pound, A Critical Appraisal.* London: Routledge and Kegan Paul, 1963.

Donoghue, Deis. *The Ordinary Universe.* London: Faber and Faber, 1968.

Drew Elizabeth. *T.S. Eliot: The Design of his Poetry.* Delhi: Doaba House, 1970.

Edwards, John Hamilton and William Vasse. *Annotated Index to the Cantos I-LXXXIV.* Berkeley: University of California Press, 1957.

Eliot, T.S. Eliot. *After Strange Gods: A Primer of Modern Heresy,* London, Faber and Faber, 1934.

—"Ezra Pound," *Poetry*, LXVIII (Sept. 1946), pp. 326-38.

—(ed.). *Ezra Pound: Selected Poems.* London: Faber and Faber, 1957.

—(ed.). *Literary Essays of Ezra Pound.* London: Faber and Faber, 1968.

—(ed.). *Literary Essays of Ezra Pound.* London: Faber and Faber, 1928.

Emery, Clark. *Ideas into Action: A Study of Pound's Cantos.* Miami: University of Miami Press, 1958.

Epsey, John J. *Ezra Pound's Mauberley: A Study in Composition.* Berkeley: University of California Press, 1955.

Feder, Lillin. *Ancient Myth in Modern Poetry.* Princeton: Princeton University Press, 1971.

Ford, Boris (ed.). *The Modern Age.* Harmondsworth: Penguin Books, 1964.

Frank, Kermode. *Romantic Image.* London: Routledge and Kegan Paul, 1966.

Fraser, G.S. *Ezra Pound.* Edinburgh: Oliver and Boyd, 1960.

— *The Modern Writer and His World.* Calcutta: Rupa & Co., 1961.

Gillie, Christopher. *Movement in English Literature 1900-40.* London: Cambridge University Press, 1975.

Glannone, Richard J. "Eliot's Portrait of Lady and Pound's Portrait d'une Femme," *Twentieth Century Literature*, 5, 3 (Oct. 1959), pp. 32.33.

Godwin, K.L. *The Influence of Ezra Pound.* London: Oxford University Press, 1966.

Gross, Harvey. *Sound and Form in Modern Poetry: A Study of Prosody from Thomas Hardy to Robert Lowell.* Ann Arbor: The University of Michigan Press, 1965.

Hamburger, Michael. *The Truth of Poetry.* Harmondsworth: Penguin Books, 1969.

Hesse, Eva (ed.). *New Approaches to Ezra Pound.* London: Faber and Faber, 1969.

Hoffman, Frederick J. *The Twenties.* New York: Collier Books, 1962.

Holder, Alan. "The Lesson of the Master: Ezra Pound and Henry James," *American Literature*, 35, (1 March, 1963), pp. 76-78.

Hollander, John (ed.). *Modern Poetry: Essay in Criticism.* New York: Oxford University Press, 1968.

Homberger, Eric. (ed.) *Ezra Pound: The Critical Heritage.* London: Routledge & Kegan Paul, 1972.

Honig, Edwin. "The Mutation of Pound," *The Kenyon Review*, XVII, 3 (Summer 1955), pp. 350-52.

Hunter, Jim (ed.). *Modern Poets.* London: Faber and Faber, 1968.

Hutchins, Patricia. "Ezra Pound and Thomas Hardy," *Southern Review,* IV, 1 (Jan. 1968), p. 99.

—*Ezra Pound's Kensington: An Exploration 1855-1913.* London: Faber and Faber, 1965.

Innes, Mary M. (tr.) *The Metamorphoses of Ovid.* Harmondsworth: Penguin Books, 1955.

Jackson, H. Thomas. *The Early Poetry of Ezra Pound.* Cambridge, Mass.: Harvard University Press, 1970.

Jones, A.R. "Notes towards a History of Imagism, An Examination of Literary Sources," *South Atlantic Quarterly,* LX, 1 (Summer 1961), pp. 262-72.

Jones, Howard Mumford and Richard M. Ludwig. *Guide to American Literature and its Backgrounds since 1890.* Cambridge, Mass.: Harvard University Press, 1972.

Kenner, Hugh. *The Poetry of Ezra Pound.* London: Faber & Faber, 1951.

—*The Pound Era.* London: Faber & Faber, 1972.

—(ed.). *The Translations of Ezra Pound,* London Faber and Faber, 1953.

—"The Rose in the Steel Dust," *Hudson Review,* III (1950-61), pp. 67-79.

—(ed.). *Paideuma,* 2, 2 (Fall 1973), pp. 203-5.

Landini, Richard G. "Vorticism and The Cantos of Ezra Pound," *Western Humanities Review,* XIV, 2 (Spring 1960), pp. 170-74.

Langbaum, Robert. *The Poetry of Experience.* London: Chatto & Windus, 1957.

Laughlin, James. "Ezra Pound's Propertius," *Sewanee Review,* (Oct.-Dec., 1938).

Leavis, F.R. *New Bearings in English Poetry.* Harmondsworth: Penguin Books, 1963.

Lewis, Leary (ed.). *Motive and Method in the Cantos.* New York: Columbia University Press, 1954.

May, Henry (ed.). *The Discontent of the Intellectuals: A Problem of the Twenties.* Chicago: Rand McNally & Co. 1963.

McCormick, John. *American Literature 1919-32: A Comperative History.* London: Routledge and Kegan Paul.

McDougal, Stuart Y. *Ezra Pound and the Trouadour Tradition.* Princeton: Princeton University Press, 1972.

McNaughton, William. "Ezra Pound's Meters and Rhythms," *PMLA* LXXVIII, 1 (March 1963), pp. 92-142.

Merchant, Paul. *The Epic.* London: Methuen Co. Ltd., 1971.

Miner, Earl. *The Japanese Tradition in British and American Literature.* Princeton: Princeton University Press, 1966.

Miner, Earl. "Pound, Haiku and the Image," *Hudson Review,* 9, 4 (Winter 1956-57).

Moore Marianne. *Predilections.* New York: The Viking Press, 1955.

Muecke, D.C. *Irony.* London: Methuen & Co. Ltd., 1971.

Nagy, N. Christoph de. *The Poetry of Ezra Pound: The Pre Imagist Stage.* Bern: Francke Verlag, 1960.

Quinn, Sister M. Bernetta. *The Metamorphic Tradition in Modern Poetry.* New York: Gordian Press, Inc., 1966.

Piage, D.D. (ed.). *The Selected Letters of Ezra Pound 1907-41.* London: Faber and Faber, 1971.

Pearce, Roy Harvey. *The Continuity of American Poetry.* Princeton: Princeton University Press, 1965.

Peralman, Daniel D. *The Barb of Time.* New York: Oxford University Press, 1969.

Pollard, Arthur. *Satire.* London: Methuen & Co. Ltd., 1971.

Port, Guy Daven. "Ezra Pound's Radiant Gists: A Reading of Cantos II & IV," *Wisconsing Studies in Contemporary Literature,* 3, 2 (Spring-Summer 1962), pp. 50-64.

Potts, Abbie Findlay. *The Elegiac Mode: Poetic Form in Wordsworth and other Elegists.* New York: Cornell University Press, 1967.

Pound, Ezra. *ABC of Reading.* London: Routledge and Sons, 1934.

—*A Draft of XXX Cantos.* London: Faber and Faber, 1930.

—*Guide to Kulchur.* London: Peter Owen, 1966.

— *How to Read.* London: Desmond Harmsworth, 1931.

—*Hugh Selwyn Mauberley.* London: The Ovid Press, 1920.

—*Imaginary Letters.* Paris: The Black Sun Press, 1930.

—Instigations, together with *the Chinese Written Character as a Medium for Poetry.* London: Faber and Faber, 1967, New York: Boni & Liveright, 1920.

Pound, Ezra. *Literary Essays of Ezra Pound,* ed. T.S. Eliot. London: Faber and Faber, 1954.

—*Make it New.* London: Faber and Faber, 1934.

—*Pavannes and Divisions.* New York: Alfred Knopf, 1918.

—*Personae: The Collected Poems of Ezra Pound.* New York: Boni and Liveright, 1926.

—*Polite Essays.* London: Faber and Faber, 1937.

—*Selected Poems,* ed. T.S. Eliot. London: Faber and Faber, 1928.

—*Selected Prose 1904-65,* ed. William Cookson, London: Faber and Faber, 1973.

—*Selected Letters of Ezra Pound 1907-41,* ed. D.D. Paige. London: Faber and Faber, 1971.

—*The Spirit of Romance.* London: Peter Owen, 1952.

—*The Translations of Ezra Pound,* Tr. Hugh Kenner. London: Faber and Faber, 1970.

Press, John. *A Map of Modern English Verse.* London: Oxford University Press, 1969.

Ramsey, Warren. "Uses of the Visible: American Imagism, French Symbolism," *Comparative Literature Studies,* IV, 1 and 2, pp. 177-79.

Rosenthal, M.L. *A Primer of Ezra Pound.* New York: MacMillan, 1960.

Ross, Robert H. *The Georgian Revolt: Rise and Fall of a Poetic Ideal 1910-22.* London: Faber and Faber, 1967.

Ruthven, KK. *A Guide to Ezra Pound's Personae (1926)* Berkeley: University of California Press, 1969.

Schneidau, Herbert N. *Ezra Pound: The Image and the Real.* Baton Rouge: Louisiana State University Press, 1969.

—"Vorticism and the Career of Ezra Pound," *Modern Philogy,* 65, 3, (Feb. 1968), pp. 215-26.

Shipley, Joseph T. (ed.). *Dictionary of World Literature.* Totoa, Littlefield, Adams & Co. 1972.

Sieburth, Richard. *Instigations, Ezra Pound and Remy de Gourmont.* Cambridge, Mass: Harvard University Press, 1978.

Sisson, C.H. *English Poetry 1900-1950.* London: Rupert Hart-Davis, 1971.

Skelton, Robin. *The Practice of Poetry.* London: Heinemann, 1971.

Slatin, Myles. "History of Pound's Cantos I-XVI," *American Literature,* 55, 2 (May 1963), pp. 183-89.

Spears, Monroe K. *Dionysus and the City: Modernism in Twentieth-Century Poetry.* London: Oxford University Press, 1970.

Spiller, Robert E (ed.). *A Time of Harvest: American Literature 1910-60.* New York: American Century Series, 1962.

Stevenson, Elizabeth. *Babbitts and Bohemians: The American 1920s.* London: The MacMillan Company, 1967.

Stock, Noel. *Reading the Cantos: A Study of Meaning in the Cantos.* London: Routledge and Kegan Paul, 1967.

Sutton, Walter. *American Free Verse: The Modern Revolution in Poetry.* New York: New Directions, 1973.

—(ed.). *Ezra Pound: A Collection of Critical Essays.* Englewood Cliffs: Prentice-Hall, 1962.

—"Mauberley, The Waste Land, and the Problem of Unified Form," *Contemporary Literature,* 9, 1 (Winter 1968), pp. 17-27.

Tatek Allen. *Reactionary Essays on Poetry and Ideas.* New York: Books for Libraries Press, 1968.

Ṭhomas, vogler A. *Preludes to Vision: The Epic Venture in Blake, Wordsworth, Keats, and Hart Crane.* Berkeley: University of California Press, 1971.

Unger, Leonard (ed.). *Seven Modern American Poets.* A.N. Wheeler & Co. (P) Ltd., 1991.

Untermeyer, Louis. *Makers of the Modern World.* New York: Simond and Schuter, 1955.

Wees, William C. "Ezra Pound as a Vorticist," *Wisconsin Studies in Contemporary Literarure,* 6, 1 (Winter Spring), pp. 57-63.

Wilson, Douglas L. *The Genteel Tradition.* Cambridge, Mass: Harvard University Press, 1967.

Witemeyer, Hugh. *The Poetry of Ezra Pound: Forms and Renewal 1908-20.* Berkeley: University of California Press, 1969.

Witham, W. Tasker. *The Adolescent in thc American Novel 1920-60.* New York: Frederuck Ungar Publishing Co., 1964.

Wright, George T. *The Poet in the Poetry: The Personage of Eliot, Yeats and Pound.* Berkeley: University of California Press, 1960.

Yip, Wai-lim. *Ezra Pound's Cathay.* Princeton: Princeton University Press, 1969.

Index